"A must read."

– Dwayne Barkman, retired pastor,
Warman, Saskatchewan

"I highly recommend this book."

– Lando Klassen, founder of House of James bookstore
Abbotsford, B.C.

"A sensitive and thought provoking read."

–Lorraine Dick, Care Ministry Assistant,
Clearbrook Mennonite Brethren Church, Abbotsford, B.C.

"A book every family will want to possess to guide them through those times."

– Norm Miller,
retired pastor, college president, professor, chaplain, and engineer

"I encourage all readers to not only read these pages, but to also accept the wisdom and support they contain."

– Scott Tolhurst, former Pastor of Clearbrook Mennonite Brethren Church,
Abbotsford B.C.

See more endorsements
at the back of the book.

Preparing to Cross the Finish Line

A Guide to Help Families and Individuals with End-of-Life Issues and Funerals

By
Walter Wiens

Mill Lake Books

Mill Lake Books
Chilliwack, BC, Canada
https://jamescoggins.wordpress.com/mill-lake-books/

Cover design by Ryan Polinsky

ISBN: 978-1-998787-01-2

Foreword

This book portrays the Christian life as a marathon, a long journey in the context of a Western, post-Christian culture. This marathon is a time in which people prepare to cross the finish line of their lives. This is a book that is thoroughly scriptural and packed with illustrations, designed to guide people through this marathon from where they are now through the challenges they will encounter as they move toward the victory ribbon.

The author, Pastor Walter Wiens, covers a wealth of life and death issues, starting from a ministry background that forms a strong foundation for this extensive and valuable document. After a pastoral ministry in Medicine Hat, Alberta, he moved on to become a chaplain at the Headingley Correctional Institution in Winnipeg, Manitoba for over thirteen years. Then he received valuable experience as a resident chaplain in Riverview Health Centre, Winnipeg, Manitoba. Since October 1, 2002, he has been the Pastor of Care Ministries in the Clearbrook Mennonite Brethren Church in Abbotsford, British Columbia, a church congregation predominantly composed of seniors. In this position, he has assisted in all levels of preparing for and officiating at more than four hundred funerals, walking with the families in their time of grief. This history of faithful ministry fully qualifies him to deliver the priceless teaching that flows through the pages of this book.

Scripturally, the marathon begins with a commitment to Christ and concludes when we come to the end of life and cross the finish life into the life beyond. Many Bible verses are used in the manuscript to provide a biblical underpinning for the subject matter.

When we are faced with our own death or the death of a loved one, there is a great need for counsel and loving guidance. When I was faced with the passing of Edna, the love of my life, my family and I became the thankful recipients of the comforting care offered by Walter and his wife Edith. As a retired pastor, it has also been my distinct privilege, not only to be an observer of Pastor Walter's ministry, but also to participate with him in conducting a fair number of funeral services. His care, compassion, and competence always came to the fore.

When death happens, there are a multitude of decisions that need to be made in a relatively short time, such as the choice of a funeral home, whether there will be a full funeral or none at all, and whether there will be a cremation or a burial. Other decisions include choosing a casket, choosing pallbearers, writing a eulogy, writing a life story, and preparing a notice for the newspaper. All of this is covered in this book.

In the course of the marathon, there might have been inner hurts and broken relationships with loved ones. These can seriously affect us at the time of a family member's death and complicate efforts to relate to one another during the planning of the funeral and during the funeral service itself. The author carefully deals with these delicate subjects at length, assuring us that healing is possible.

Most importantly, the author delves deeply into the spiritual preparation that needs to happen as we move toward the culmination of the spiritual marathon. Is there a way of finding assurance that we will actually cross the finish line to the glorious life beyond? There is a whole chapter in this book dealing with that subject, helping the reader to find assurance and peace.

Preparing to Cross the Finish Line is a book that every lay person and every member of the clergy should read in order to effectively run the Christian marathon themselves and to help others along the way.

– Art Isaac

Art Isaac served for twelve years in full-time pastorates and over twenty years in part-time ministries, as well as many years in church leadership. He is now enjoying full retirement, living with his children in Harrison Hot Springs, B.C. Art is a deeply loved mentor to the author.

Acknowledgements

As I reflect on this book, I am fully aware of my indebtedness to many people. When I begin to express thanks, I am aware that I will omit many people who had a part in the writing of this book.

I begin by expressing thanks to the many families I have had the sacred opportunity to walk with in their valley of loss and grief. Recognizing that each funeral service is a solemn journey with a family, I acknowledge that my heart has repeatedly been touched with grace and compassion.

I also wish to express my thanks and dedicate this book to the funeral directors who have partnered with me as we walked with grieving families. May God's compassion and wisdom fill and empower you to do this very important, yet often criticized, ministry for our fellow citizens.

I further wish to express my thanks particularly to several individuals who have given suggestions and helpful observations in the writing of this book in its various stages. As I recognize these people, I know I will unknowingly omit some people. Pastor Dwayne Barkman, my brother-in-law, not only provided observations on the first drafts of this book but also shared many conversations on pastoral ministry. The comments by Dwayne and his wife Irma were both instructive and encouraging. Rev. Norman Miller encouraged me to provide a broader church perspective, particularly as it pertained to funeral messages and burial words. Lando Klassen, founder of the House of James, a Christian bookstore, directed me to valuable resources, critiqued the manuscript, and encouraged me with the words that a book such as this one was much needed. When Vi Wiens became aware that I was writing this book, she stressed the value of it and encouraged me to speak with boldness and clarity in critical areas. Don Balzer, as a retired pastor, stressed the need for this book and challenged me to address some difficult areas.

It has been a sacred opportunity for my wife and me to share life with Art Isaac, and earlier with his dear wife Edna before God called her home. We value Art as a dear friend, but also as a wise spiritual father. Therefore, I have invited his input and suggestions and am grateful that he has accepted my invitation to write a Foreword to this book.

The person who has helped in ways too numerous to note in the writing of this book is David Giesbrecht. When I shared that I had a vision to write a book on helping people prepare to cross the finish line, David generously requested that he help me fulfill this vision. Over a period of more than five years, he has encouraged me to persevere, meeting regularly with me to check my progress and reading and critiquing the numerous drafts. David introduced me to Robert Martens and Jim Coggins. Robert Martens checked on the many small details that ensured the book would be presented in the best form, and Jim Coggins took the final manuscript and developed it into a book format.

I also wish to recognize Ryan Polinsky, who patiently provided numerous drafts of the book cover. Ryan, thank you for your creativity and perseverance in artistically displaying what it means to cross the finish line of life and be with Jesus.

The person who has had the greatest impact on my life, and therefore on the writing of this book, is my wife Edith. There are several areas in which I wish to express my gratitude to Edith. First, Edith has encouraged me through the numerous phases of our lives—seminary training, walking together in pastoral ministry, and particularly the times when I led families in their valleys of loss and grief. At times, I did not believe this book would ever come to completion; at those times, Edith urged that we take another vacation/study break to continue the hard work of writing. Her encouragement is a major reason this book has finally reached completion. Therefore, I gladly give my warmest thankyou to Edith, my soul mate for over 53 years. As I thank Edith, I wish to recognize with humility and deepest gratitude our children and their spouses, Andrew and Sara as well as Amy and Keith.

– Walter Wiens

Table of Contents

Preface...11

Introduction and Overview...15

Chapter One: Being with People as They Cross the Finish Line...................21

Chapter Two: The Need for a Funeral Service................................25

Chapter Three: The Need to Plan a Funeral Service........................29
    1. Plan as a Family
    2. Preplanning Funeral Services
    3. Preplanning while You Still Can
    4. Selecting a Funeral Home
    5. Planning Reveals Our Core Values

Chapter Four: Parts in a Funeral Service..45
    1. Naming of the Service
    2. Viewing
    3. Flowers
    4. Donations in Memory of a Loved One
    5. Obituary/Eulogy/Life Story/Tributes
    6. Children
    7. Bulletins
    8. Hymns, Spiritual Songs, and Special Music

Chapter Five: Burial Service, Interment or Committal Service.............63
    1. Parts of a Burial Service
    2. Coffins
    3. Pallbearers
    4. Special Items in a Burial Service

Chapter Six: Recognizing Family Brokenness.................................71

Chapter Seven: Writing Our Life Story: A Personal and a Faith Legacy......75
    1. Principles and Values that Should Determine Our Approach
    2. Guidelines for Writing Life Stories

Chapter Eight: Assurance That We Will Cross the Finish Line
to Eternal Life 83
    1. A Believer in Jesus Is Assured to Cross the Finish Line
    2. A Follower of Jesus Is Assured to Cross the Finish Line
    3. Those Who Look Forward to the Prize Jesus Has for Them
        Are Assured to Cross the Finish Line.
    4. A Lover of Jesus (His Bride) Is Assured to Cross the Finish Line

Chapter Nine: Restoring Hope and Acceptance of the Present
as We Near the Finish Line 91
    1. Enjoy the Present—It Is a Gift of God
    2. Accept the Present with Gratitude
    3. Trust in God's Constant Care, Right to the End
Chapter Ten: Restoring Peace in Relationships as We Near
the Finish Line 99
    1. Why Bother Restoring Broken Relationships?
    2. How Can I Have the Strength to Pursue Restoration when
       My Health Is Failing?
    3. Preliminary Thoughts on Restoring Relationships
    4. Classes of Broken Relationships
    5. Restoring Peace within the Family
Chapter Eleven: Running the Race and Crossing the Finish Line
in Community...117
    1. An Acknowledgment that We Live in an Individualistic Society
    2. Weep with Those who Weep
    3. The Balance between Supporting and Empowering/Resourcing
    4. A Society's Care for the Weak and Vulnerable
    5. The Various Models of Living in Community
    6. Are We Our Elders' Keepers?
    7. Mentoring: Valuing the Wisdom and Blessings of Our Elderly
Appendices...129
    Appendix A: Writing a Personal Life Story
    Appendix B: Forms Provided by a Church
    Appendix C: Legal and Financial Matters
    Appendix D: Health Matters
    Appendix E: Necessary Information
    Appendix F: Definitions
    Appendix G: Selected Books on Aging and the End of Life

Preface

The Psalmist prayed that God would not cast him away and forsake him when he was old and his strength was gone. Jesus implored his closest disciples to stay with him as he knew his greatest time of need was near. These two calls for help and for support, uttered years ago by the Psalmist and by Jesus, are expressed by many older people.

This means that what I wish to address in this book is not a

> "Do not cast me away when I am old; do not forsake me when my strength is gone" (Psalm 71:9).
> "He (Jesus) took Peter and the two sons of Zebedee along with him, and he began to be sorrowful and troubled. Then he said to them, 'My soul is overwhelmed with sorrow to the point of death. Stay here and keep watch with me'" (Matthew 26:37-38).

new phenomenon. My desire is to speak to the topic of walking with people in their final stage of life, helping them as they make key decisions. My goal is to do so from a biblical and theological framework that deals with practical issues and also speaks to our current cultural environment. I have sensed a growing conviction to write on these issues as I have walked with elderly people and their families. God has led me on a particular path in my faith journey. In this faith journey, I have perceived a sensitivity to older people and therefore how best to be present with them.

On this journey as a pastor, God has given my wife and me the privilege of walking with individuals at various stages and circumstances of life. Following a thirteen-year period of being Jesus to inmates in a correctional institution, I was a resident chaplain in the Riverview Health Centre, Winnipeg, Manitoba. This gave me a greater understanding of, and compassion for, elderly people. It gave me more familiarity with how best to walk with the residents in their final years—even months, days, and hours—of life. We sensed that God was directing our ministry focus to be with elderly people.

Therefore, the next key milestone in our lives seemed very natural. This was when my wife and I discerned God's leading to serve as a pastoral couple in a church in British Columbia. This congregation consists mostly of elderly people. Then, after serving about ten years—walking with individuals in their final years and months and planning many funerals—I again discerned God speaking to me, saying, "Walter, I have called you and your wife into this care ministry with elderly people. I want you to reflect deeper on what is involved in caring for elderly people."

In response, I did three specific things. First, I purchased and read books that dealt with elderly people. (These books are included in the resources at the end of this book.) Second, I took three summer courses at Regent College on understanding the needs of elderly people. Third, I took a vacation that was actually a study break where my goal was to read and study the broad area of serving older people.

In this vacation/study break, I read and then began writing observations and reflections on various aspects of caring for older people. After reading and reflecting for several days, I felt God's Spirit nudge me to also write down what I had learned from helping families with funerals. I had often heard from family members that they had wished that a basic manual on planning a funeral was available. When I shared the vision of this guide book, various individuals recommended that I divide this book into two sections: one for elderly people and their families, and the other for pastors who are walking with elderly people.

The initial scope of the manuscript was limited to helping people plan funerals. However, as I wrote down my experiences and read about the various facets of preparing funerals, I became aware that the funeral and burial are only one aspect of the final steps of our lives. I envision our lives as a marathon and our funeral and burial as marking our crossing the finish line. The title of this book expresses my goal to help people prepare to cross their finish line. But the more I reflected on the scope of the book, the more I became aware that a person's preparedness to "cross the finish line" needs to begin long before a person starts to make funeral preparations. In fact, we always need to be prepared to "cross the finish line."

> Four of the first books that informed me on the critical issues facing elderly people and challenged me to respond with a biblical perspective are:
> • Stanley Hauerwas, Carole Bailey Stoneking, Keith G. Meador, and David Cloutier, eds. *Growing Old in Christ*.
> • James M. Houston and Michael Parker. *A Vision for the Aging Church: Renewing Ministry for and by Seniors*.
> • Fred Craddock, Dale Goldsmith, and Joy V. Goldsmith. *Speaking of Dying: Recovering the Church's Voice in the Face of Death*.
> • Allen Verhey. *The Christian Art of Dying: Learning from* Jesus.

This begs the questions: "What is involved in being prepared? How can I be prepared?" These questions can be answered on several levels. These levels involve relationships—with God, with people, and with ourselves. I begin with the premise that the core identity that makes us human is that we are relational beings. This means that we are fully alive and fully prepared to cross the finish line when all our relationships are right. In this book, I will touch on principles as well as practical steps that will help us in our relationships—with God, with people, and with ourselves.

"LORD, who may dwell in your sanctuary? Who may live on your holy hill?... Who may ascend the hill of the LORD? Who may stand in his holy place?" (Psalm 15:1, 24:3). The Psalmist's answers to these questions confirm that a person's relationship with God will be evident in his character and actions.

I recognize that some people maintain that a person needs only to be in a right relationship with God to be prepared to cross the finish line. In other words, they believe that when they have made peace with God, they are then prepared to die. I am convinced that a person's right relationship with God impacts this person's relationship with other people, and certainly with himself. Therefore, the scope of this book needs to be more than what might be perceived by some people as the core requirement to be prepared to cross the finish line: stepping from life on earth to life with God in heaven.

This book applies to any individual who is becoming older, as well as to this person's family. Each chapter is concluded with summary thoughts, reflections, and often a challenge, as well as a prayer. My goal is that this book will not only be a source of helpful information, but also a guide that will inspire personal reflection and action.

Introduction and Overview

"Death be not proud, though some have called thee Mighty and
dreadfull, for, thou art not soe,
For, those, whom thou think'st, thou dost overthrow,
Die not, poore death, nor yet canst thou kill mee...
One short sleep past, wee wake eternally,
And death shall be no more; death, thou shalt die."
— *John Donne, "Holy Sonnet X"*

This book is dedicated to elderly individuals and their children or friends and families.

Are you an older person or senior who wants to begin writing some ideas that you wish to be part of your funeral service? Your last will and testament is in place, but do you have questions about your funeral details? Do you find yourself asking questions such as the following:

• What funeral home should I choose?
• What should I include in my life story?
• What special items would I like in my funeral service?

If you are thinking ahead to your own funeral, this book is for you.

Are you an adult son or daughter of a mother or father who has just died? I had met with an adult son and other family members to plan his mother's funeral service. As the son left our meeting, he stopped me and commented, "Before I came here to plan mother's service, I had no idea what had to be done. The church should provide a booklet on the basic things involved in planning a funeral service." Do any of the following apply to you:

• Do you wish that your elderly mother would talk to you about her funeral desires?

• Are you not sure how to bring up the topic of a parent's funeral or something else you really want to talk about?

• Do you know that you will be responsible to plan the funeral service of a loved one?

This book is for you!

Here is an overview of the book:

Chapter One: Being with People as They Cross the Finish Line

As we begin thinking about the funeral service, there will be other matters that come to our mind. Looking at the parts involved in a funeral service might be compared to looking in a mirror. As we note the items we will take care of in the funeral, our spirit will remind us of things we believe we will want to attend to or at least things we will be prompted to consider. Recognizing that this will happen, this book is not only devoted to help you plan a funeral service. The planning for a funeral service must include more than the specific details of the service. As will become evident, we can only properly plan a funeral service when other details of life are taken care of. This book is for all of us who are in the last stage of life. Yet, since we know that none of us lives in isolation from other people, this book is also for those who walk with elderly people—parents, aunts, uncles, and friends. The book begins with a recognition that walking with people in their final moments brings about an awareness of the sacredness of life. This also means that we will want to embrace and treat the moments before and after death not only with sensitivity and compassion but also with courage and wisdom.

Chapter Two: The Need for a Funeral Service

The need for a funeral service is based on the premise that our lives and our deaths matter because we are of value. Therefore, when we cross the finish line, a funeral is needed as an occasion for grief and thanksgiving, for recognizing our loss and acknowledging God and his compassion, presence, and wisdom in our lives and the lives of our loved ones.

Chapter Three: The Need to Plan a Funeral Service

It follows naturally that there is a need to plan the funeral service. This chapter emphasizes that this planning should best be done together with the loved one and the family, so that the wishes of all are considered.

Chapter Four: Parts in a Funeral Service

Chapter Four introduced the various parts in a funeral service. This chapter begins with considering the name of the service: is it a funeral, a memorial service, or a celebration of life? Then, the chapter goes on to address items such as viewing the body, flowers, donations, music, the life story, and the bulletin.

Chapter Five: Burial Service, Interment, or Committal Service

Chapter Five presents the parts of a burial service, addressing matters such as the selection of a coffin and meaningful practices that a family might want to include in a burial service.

Chapter Six: Recognizing Family Brokenness

Chapter Six presents the likelihood and therefore the challenge that the death of a loved one and the ensuing funeral service might be an occasion that will expose family brokenness and heartache. As we become aware of this brokenness, we will not want to ignore the difficulties. But we will want to receive God's grace and also extend his grace to others with a goal of bringing healing.

Chapter Seven: Writing Our Life Story

In chapter Seven, the focus is on our life story. The purpose of a life story is that it be an honest expression of our faith journey with God. We will want to write our life story with the goal that God be glorified. We will do so by providing an open account of our brokenness and of God's faithfulness. Another goal of our life story is that those who hear and read the life story will be given hope that God can similarly be gracious to them in their failures and waywardness.

Chapter Eight: Assurance that We will Cross the Finish Line to Eternal Life

This chapter deals with being assured that when we cross the finish line, we will have eternal life. This chapter is based on the premise that being prepared to cross the finish line from this life to eternal life with Jesus for all eternity includes much more than making the funeral arrangements. We must have a restored relationship with God. This is possible only through faith expressed by obedience to Jesus. We will only have complete peace with God when we have peace with all the people he has placed next to us in our relationships.

Chapter Nine: Restoring Hope and Acceptance of the Present as We Near the Finish Line

This chapter is about the reality that, as we near the end of life, we might despair and have difficulty accepting the hard realities around us. Towards the end of life, the challenges and trials might increase. Therefore, when we are tempted to give up and despair, we need to accept what is happening because we believe our lives, with all our trials included, are lived under God. We appreciate that marathon runners can sometimes become discouraged and lose hope as they reach the end of the race. Similarly, we might have doubts about whether we will make it to the end of life. Yes, we might have peace with God, but as we come to the end of life, our sense of hope and peace might be lacking or at least diminishing. We can easily become discouraged. In this chapter, my goal is to restore hope, even when life seems to crash in with many trials and difficulties.

Chapter Ten: Restoring Peace in Relationships as We Near the Finish Line

Chapter Ten recognizes that relationships might be broken and we are called to restore them. The ultimate reason we must take the trouble to restore relationships is that God took the trouble to restore humankind to himself. As God's followers who have been reconciled to him, we should do all we can to restore relationships. The focus in this chapter is to provide direction that will help restore peace with other people. I believe we will only be fully prepared to cross the finish line when all our relationships are restored.

Chapter Eleven: Running the Race and Crossing the Finish Line in Community

Chapter Eleven looks at an aspect that is often overlooked. In the first ten chapters, we focused on the necessary preparations each of us needs to make to ensure we will cross the finish line. But, as we know from any Olympic marathon, there are many people who are supporting, encouraging, and helping each runner successfully run her or his race. This closing chapter is about the need for community as we run the last lap of life and cross the finish line. None of us is independent and self-sufficient. We need one another in all phases of life. This is especially evident in the final phase of life, our last lap in our life marathon. Even though we recognize that seniors are responsible to be prepared to cross the finish line, with all the areas that are included in that responsibility, we need to provide another emphasis. This emphasis is that the family, the church, and the community are also responsible for the welfare of seniors, particularly as they become frail and vulnerable in the last lap of the marathon of their lives.

Reflections

The metaphor of a marathon—and specifically the last phase before crossing the finish line—fits our lives. In the beginning of a marathon, the runners demonstrate strength and resolve. But as the runners near the finish line, they might be completely exhausted and even unsure whether they will be able to make it across the finish line. The spectators will cheer on the runners, encouraging them to endure and give their best. Even though the runners are frail—and some might even be so exhausted that they can barely crawl across the finish line—each runner is still cheered and valued. Yet, do we do the same for one another as we approach the end of our lives? No one would ever suggest a runner has less dignity and worth because the runner is extremely weak and can barely stumble through the last part of the race. Yet, do we give one another less dignity as we become frail and sick toward the end of our lives? As every runner in a marathon deserves recognition, so every person deserves a service of remembrance. In this book, we will reflect on how we can best honor one another as we run the marathon of life and finally cross the finish line.

Prayer

Our heavenly Father, with the psalmist David, we pray, "O LORD, you have searched us, and you know us....All the days ordained for us were written in your book before one of them came to be. How precious to us are your thoughts, O God." We honor you as our God who knows each of our days and who cares deeply for us. May our recognition of you and your love impact how we perceive our lives. Also, may this awareness of you be evident as we reflect on our lives and our loved ones' lives. May you receive all honor and praise as we reflect on our lives and then plan and provide funeral services. All honor belongs to you—in life and in death. In Jesus' name, Amen.

Chapter One
Being with People as They Cross the Finish Line

In the Introduction, I noted that our lives can be compared to a marathon that begins at birth and concludes as we cross the finish line at death. I further mentioned that there is nothing more important for any of us than to be ready for the moment when we cross the finish line.

Several times, God has graciously given me the privilege of being present at that most sacred moment when a dear person took her or his last breath. My wife Edith and I, along with her sister, stood around her father's bed as he was drawing his last breath. His spirit was with us one moment, and the next moment he was with Jesus.

Several years earlier, while I was a resident chaplain at Riverview Health Centre in Winnipeg, Manitoba, a husband requested that I stay with him as his wife neared death and to be with them as she died. Another time, a friend in Abbotsford, British Columbia, asked that Edith and I be with him as the hospital monitors showed life slowly ebbing away from his wife. On numerous occasions, we have stood with family members, holding hands, reading Bible promises, and expressing God's comfort, just hours before a loved one was called home to heaven. At other times, families have asked that we join them at the bedside of a loved one who had died.

On one particular occasion, I sensed God's Spirit directing me to visit a dying member of our church. When my wife and I entered his room, his wife was sitting next to his bed. After I took the seat beside his wife, she looked up at her husband and noted, "He just passed away." God called this elderly man home at the very minute that we walked into his room. We were able to be present to care for his wife as she faced a future without her husband, who had passed away in our presence, this time without us being aware that this was God's moment to take a saint home.

These sacred moments have changed how we perceive funerals. A close friend shared that he also has a new perception of death after he was present as his wife passed away. He wrote that his wife's passing from here to glory was the first occasion he had witnessed someone's death. It was a very sacred moment but also very traumatic, as he realized he was now alone. His life's partner was gone. (In this book I am using the word "funeral" to refer to celebration of life services, memorial services and funerals. Later, I will note the distinction between these terms.)

God has also given me the opportunity to plan and lead many funerals. Walking with families during these sacred moments has left a deep impression on my heart, and I thank God for this. I recognize these to be holy moments. Therefore, I remind myself of Paul's words to Timothy: "Do your best to present yourself to God as one approved, a workman who does not need to be ashamed and who correctly handles the word of truth" (2 Timothy 2:15). This means that even though I have planned many funerals and have also been with individuals in those sacred moments as they take their last breath, I need to realize in a greater manner than ever the solemnity of life and the seriousness of death. Therefore, in Paul's words, I want to do my best before God since I am God's workman.

Even while I accept my commitment to do my best as I write this book, I identify with the Apostle Paul's testimony, "But we have this treasure in jars of clay to show that this all-surpassing power is from God and not from us" (2 Corinthians 4:7). I use this testimony from the Apostle Paul to make clear that I am placing my frailty over against the magnificence and enormity of the topic of this book. I identify with J. Todd Billings, who recognized his inability to comprehend the subject matter in his book, *The End of the Christian Life*. He acknowledged his frailty with the words, "I write as an act of pilgrimage, I cannot possibly master the realities about which I speak in this book—the mysteries of death and new life, and his gospel among crumbling mortals....In speaking of God, I speak of One whom I cannot comprehend. As Augustine of Hippo stated boldly in the fourth century, 'If you have been able to comprehend it, you have comprehended something else instead of God'" (Billings, 17).

When I began this book, my focus was primarily on the practical steps to be followed in planning a funeral and burial service. Yet, the longer I reflect on this topic, the more I realize these practical directions can never be fully adequate nor will they ever do justice to the subject matter—being present during the final moments before death, experiencing the death of a loved one, pondering how to remember a loved one, and then preparing for this solemn moment. What began as writing a "manual" on preparing to cross the finish line has shifted to reflecting on the most sacred and solemn moments in any person's life. I trust that an awareness of the magnificence and grandeur of the topic will be evident in my writing.

Just as the Apostle Paul described humans as "jars of clay," I point to the fact that the word "humanity" has as its root in "humus," "which means "of the earth." In this book I am reflecting that we who are "of the earth" will eventually return to the earth. But we also have in us the breath of God; we are created in his image. We who are mortal will be immortal; we who are of the earth will be clothed with a heavenly body. Our "finish line" is not when we return to the earth. Our lives will continue through all eternity. This places a different perspective on being prepared for the day we cross the finish line.

Reflections

Within a span of a year, we will watch thousands of violent acts on the news. This can lead us to become callous to the finality of death and even to the tragedy of cruel acts of murder and violence. We need to stop and take a moment to consider the solemn and sacred moment when God takes breath away. Ponder these questions:

• How have I been present when a loved one passed away? What emotions did I feel?

• How have I walked with a loved one who is becoming weaker with a terminal disease?

• When an individual is near the end of life, how do I remain present with this person?

Prayer

Father God, in a world of violence and cruel and murderous deaths, may I see life and death through your lens. May I sense the preciousness of every moment. May I be grateful for all you give—for each moment of life. May I fully cherish the gift of life. In the name of Jesus, who is the resurrection and the life, Amen.

Chapter Two
The Need for a Funeral Service

Some years ago, an elderly man in our church expressed this thought: "You don't need to have any funeral service for me." This man had been active in our church; he had a loving family as well as many friends. As his death drew near, a good number of his friends had already passed away. Since I was acquainted with this man, I knew he would have felt their loss and been present at their funeral services. He was weak and frail in his last months and weeks. The family found it difficult and not easy to hear these words given right at the end of a dear husband's and father's grueling last days.

How was this family to respond to this request? Throughout his lifetime, this man had fully participated in life. His family recognized that these words were said because he was frail, full of pain, and discouraged. He spoke out of his depression and misery.

The family chose to honor his request. But they also knew their mother and the children and grandchildren would be devastated if they could not honor a dear husband, father, and grandfather. Therefore, they did not have a normal funeral service, but they had a short service as part of a reception. They had many good memories and shared them at the luncheon.

In this man's situation, his words were not consistent with the rest of his life. He had always thought of others and would do what was best for his family and friends. His final wish was therefore not in keeping with his character.

However, the trend not to have any form of a service where family, friends, and other people can gather is becoming more frequent in our Western society. A family might place a short obituary in the newspaper and then add the words, "No service by request."

We ask, "Why would individuals not desire that family and friends have a funeral service for themselves?" or "Why would a family not want to have a funeral service for one of its members—a father, a mother, a sibling, or even a child?"

Another perplexing phenomenon, at least for me, is that people will attend or watch a memorial service for a celebrity, a famous actor, or a slain police officer, but they will not plan a service where their family and friends can attend their own funeral. Does it bother us that we will watch the televised funeral of someone we don't know over TV, but we will not be able to attend a funeral of a close friend we have known for years—just because the family will not plan a service for their father or mother? What if the family of a police officer who was shot, or the family of a political leader who died while in office, stated, "No service by request." Would our response be, "That can't be done. The city or the country must provide a service for her or him"? We think it is inconceivable that a well-known politician or celebrity or slain police officer would not be given a public funeral. Yet, how can we then not provide a public funeral where others can express their love and respect for us or our loved one?

Answers to these questions need to draw us to our knees. How we view the dead, our loved ones, and our own death, is one of the greatest tests of our society—and of us individually. Thomas Lynch wrote, "A failure to deal authentically with death may have something to do with an inability to deal authentically with life" (Thomas G. Long and Thomas Lynch, *The Good Funeral*, 60).

In the first chapter, I compared our lives to a marathon. In any marathon, two things occur when a runner crosses the finish line. First, the runner will celebrate that he or she made it to the end. The celebration might be very muffled and feeble because the runner is extremely exhausted. Yet, there will be a sense of, "I made it. At times, I did not know that I could, but I finally crossed the finish line." Second, the spectators, and certainly the runner's family and friends, will celebrate that the runner crossed the finish line.

An underlying premise in this book is that our lives and our deaths matter because we matter. Crossing the finish line is an occasion to celebrate. I believe all of us should have a sense of victory and of pride in completing a long life and should want those who knew and loved us to acknowledge this. Also, since our lives matter, a natural response is that those who know us will want to stop and recognize our lives—and therefore their loss. This means that crossing the finish line is also an occasion to grieve. Funerals are the natural response we should have to the death of every person.

If there is any doubt in our minds, or in the minds of our family, whether a funeral is needed or worthwhile, may I ask the more basic question: "Do we matter? Do we matter to ourselves and to our families and friends?" The answers to these questions are an absolute and undeniable, "Yes!" Therefore, the next question is, "How do we go about planning a funeral service?"

Reflection
Have I ever thought:
• Why should my family have a funeral service for me?
• Why not just bury me and get it over with?
• Why not just burn me up and scatter my ashes?
Certainly, there will be moments when I am discouraged and feel insignificant and unimportant. However, may I always realize that I do matter.

Prayer
Father God, I turn my eyes up to you—and then I recognize my worth. May I never accept the notions that I do not matter and that a funeral is unnecessary, pointless, and an unwarranted effort and expense. May I see my worth through your eyes. In Jesus, who expressed his worth in me by being a human person and by dying for me, Amen.

Chapter Three
The Need to Plan a Funeral Service

1. Plan as a Family

From my observation, most families plan funerals together. They will do all they can to draw everyone into the planning. When they gather to plan their mother's or father's service, they listen to one another. As they plan, the passing of their parent is still very painful. The grief is deep. They gather to comfort one another. Then they meet together with their mother's or father's pastor. They listen to one another, committed to planning a service that will honor their parent, glorify God, and unite their family. Often the family members will phone, email, or text the siblings who cannot be present to help plan the service. They do their best to include all the family members in the decisions made. Those present are committed to the goal that everyone will reach agreement on all the decisions—decisions they hope will honor their parent, maintain unity, and restore broken or fragile relationships.

When a family does not plan together the details involved in the funeral and the related issues at end of life, regretful and negative

> **Who is Responsible?**
> Who is responsible to process the funeral details? The answer will depend on various factors. Some people are of the opinion that only immediate children should be involved in the planning of a service, along with all the details. They extend this argument to other decisions, such as the distribution of a parent's belongings. In this case, the extended family members and the in-laws are not involved in key decisions. Regardless of what decision is made, the question of who is responsible to plan a funeral needs to be answered. It is important that the answer draw the family members together rather than tear them apart.

consequences will occur. I cannot emphasize strongly enough that there be coordinated planning in which the desires of all the family members are considered and heard. Grieving families should listen to one another.

Sadly, I recall several painful occasions when families did not plan together, listen to each other, or attempt to bring about reconciliation and unity. On one occasion, the family had just returned from the cemetery and was assembling prior to entering the sanctuary for the memorial service. I noticed that one family member, a daughter-in-law, was distressed. I asked her what the problem was. With the family standing nearby in scattered groups, she blurted out with intense antagonism, "He (the oldest son, her brother-in-law) did it again. He always does it. As the oldest in the family, he has never considered how anyone else wants anything. This happened at the burial. This is happening in the service. He never thinks of anyone else but himself. He never asks for anyone else's opinions or desires." I knew that, as the oldest son, he was within his legal rights as the family executor. And I had just led the burial service and was about to lead the funeral service. But I had been unaware that the family members had not all been fully consulted and everyone's wishes considered. It would have been so much better and wiser if he had listened to the other family members and taken their desires into consideration.

> **The Role of Executor**
> As an executor planning a funeral, we have an option:
> • We can insist on using our authority and power; or
> • We can give priority to our family's unity and the welfare of each member.

Very likely, unless there will be a humble and complete reconciliation, this rift within the family will remain and widen. This sister-in-law might never get over the painful events at the funeral service. However, within minutes of this incident, the family would walk together for the memorial service of their mother, would sit as a unit, and would present the appearance of being a united family. This brother-in-law would talk about his mother in glowing terms as an extremely divided family listened.

I have also observed the disappointment and even resentment when some family members refuse to change their plans for the sake of the larger family. These questions, spoken or unspoken, will continue to fester underneath the surface: "Which is more important—one family member's personal priorities (such as a scheduled vacation, work, or other commitments) or setting that aside for the good of the whole family? Why did a member not make the effort and undertake the necessary travel arrangements to be at a parent's funeral?" The opposite questions are: "What will family members sacrifice for the welfare of the larger family? How important is family?"

This can go the other way as well. When a vacation plan or another important appointment has already been made and is difficult to change, those planning the service should be considerate to the people who have these significant commitments.

I remember meeting with the loved ones of a parent. They had had a very close relationship with the parent but, as stepchildren, were not involved in the funeral details. Yet they had scheduled a two-week vacation the day after their mother passed away. In this case, the family members who were the executors considered the wishes of the family members and scheduled the memorial service for after the other members returned. Being thoughtful in planning a funeral is always the best choice.

Regrettably, heartrending pain is felt when family conflict surfaces in the planning and implementing of a funeral. Hurts that are inflicted at a funeral service go deep. Families can never redo a memorial service. The person in charge of the funeral service might have gotten his or her way, and the service

> The need to decide quickly on the date of a funeral service is taken away when the body will be embalmed or cremated. The only time there is an urgency to plan a service shortly after death is when there will be a burial service and the body will not be embalmed.

might have gone according to this person's plan, but the hurt and the division will only become deeper when other family members are ignored. My appeal to anyone responsible for funeral planning is: "Do not insist on your own way. If you are in charge of planning the funeral service, you also have an opportunity to bring about healing and unity. This is a time to extend grace and forgiveness. This is a time to listen and put other people's wishes before your own."

In the many funerals I have helped to plan, there is one constant challenge—the date of the service. Very likely no date will suit everyone. Planners should attempt to delay making a final decision until all the key people will have had their input. With the practices of embalming and cremation becoming more common, funerals can be delayed. However, friends and extended family members might then question why a certain date was selected, particularly when it is three or more weeks after a person died. The key issue is that the selected date was agreed on by all the family members and that the decision maintained, supported, and strengthened unity in the family.

I wish to give a final word on the importance of healing and unity within a family at the time of a funeral. The death of a loved one might not come at the right time. There may be "unfinished business" that the person whose funeral is being planned wished had been done or other people believe should have been dealt with. Family members might have similar issues—such as, feelings of regret that they did not do more. There might be regrets about missed opportunities with the loved one who passed away or unfinished business with other family members that has surfaced.

May I highlight two things: a promise as well as an appeal. The promise is that "The LORD is gracious and righteous; our God is full of compassion" (Psalm 116:5). With the Psalmist, we need to trust that our God—the God we believe in and the God of the people with whom we may have a conflict—"is full of compassion." God is aware of any "unfinished business," involving both the deceased person and the people who remain. May we hold on to God's promise and his character, understanding that the Lord is gracious. We can and must trust his grace.

The appeal is that we seek to bring about reconciliation and peace within our families. Neither we nor our loved ones will have completed everything that we or they wished. We will want to be gracious towards each other. In this regard, I am drawn to Jesus' commendation: "It will be good for that servant whose master finds him doing so when he returns" (Matthew 24:46). Jesus' approval does not depend on us having completed all our work. His approval is dependent upon our commitment to him. In other words, we may never succeed in bringing about full harmony within our families. God will bless us when we seek to bring reconciliation, when we seek to bring peace as Jesus taught in Matthew 5:9: "Blessed are the peacemakers, for they will be called the sons of God." God's blessing will rest upon us as we seek peace in our family. (The importance of recognizing conflict and striving to bring about reconciliation is dealt with in greater detail in Chapter Six, "Recognizing Family Brokenness," and Chapter Ten, "Restoring Peace in Relationships as We Near the Finish Line.")

2. Preplanning Funeral Services

Planning funeral services ahead of time is a person's expression of love to his or her family members. Before I explain the matter of planning a funeral service in further detail and explain the value of doing so, I will note an author whom I respect who takes the opposite view. Thomas G. Long argues that there is a negative element in preplanning one's funeral and suggests that all preplanning should be "held like a thistle, very gently." He is referring to items such as the hymns, the Scripture, and the choice between burial and cremation. He questions the desire to pin down the details of one's own funeral. He asks, "Why would we want to do that? Either we don't want our families making those decisions, so we decide to stay in control from beyond the grave....More commonly, we don't want to be a burden on our family. Truthfully, though, bearing one another's burdens makes us human and brings us closer to the spirit of Christ....We don't want to deprive our loved ones of the soul-making labor of fulfilling the law of Christ by bearing our burdens in a time of need" (Thomas G. Long, *Accompany Them with Singing*, 181-182).

I will not respond fully to the various parts of Thomas Long's argument except to say that when a person preplans her or his service, this person is fulfilling the law of Christ by bearing the burden of his or her children in the time of their grief and loss. In every loving family, the children will want to bear these burdens as they express their love for their parents. As I describe aspects of preplanning, it should become clear that this is usually not a matter of controlling from beyond the grave but of caring for loved ones.

I encourage children to approach their parents and bring up the topic of planning a funeral service. All the details following the death of a loved one take planning and preparation. Will the decisions be made at a time of intense loss and grief, moments after a parent has died? Or will the decisions be made, or at least contemplated, at a time when children and parents can calmly consider all the factors?

In the situation where a couple has no children, I encourage the couple to approach their siblings or close friends. If there is hesitancy on the part of an elderly couple who have no children to discuss their plan, here again it is the loving thing for those nearest to them to approach them thoughtfully. Decisions will need to be made. Will they be made according to their wishes and with their input?

This also applies to a person who is not married. I encourage this person to initiate a conversation with other family members or close friends.

A principle applies here as in all the other circumstances: to not make decisions and plans is to make a decision. The decision is that, when a person does not make any plans, the planning will be made by other people, who will need to agree on and determine core items quickly, often in a state of grief.

If you are the aging person, who will make the decisions? Possibly, you have several specific desires for your funeral. You might want favorite songs or special readings to be included in the service or printed in the bulletin. Does anyone know? Have you written these wishes down, and do your children or the people who will plan your funeral know where your wishes can be found?

I commend people who come to my office to process the various aspects of planning their own funeral service. Normally, these people have made arrangements with a funeral director. They will usually have their will in place. When their family hears that their parent has died, there will certainly be grief. But, in their emotional state of grief, the family will be much more able to cope with their grief if the parent has recorded specific requests and directives. When the parent has preplanned many details, then the grieving children simply need to implement the decisions that were made earlier. I can give many illustrations of the significance of preplanning a funeral service and recording the requests and decisions. I will give just two.

The first illustration happened when my wife and I travelled to Desert Hot Springs to spend time at a mobile home park. Most of the residents were "snowbirds." On our first day, we celebrated a memorial supper for a resident in this park. This resident had instructed her son and daughter to hold her memorial supper at a time when most of the "snowbirds" were present. The son and daughter lived a considerable distance from their mother's home. As the son shared memories about his mother, he emphasized two things. First, his mother had taken care of all the necessary details, and therefore all that he and his sister had needed to do as they came to be with their mother in her final weeks was to be present with her and show her love. He was very grateful that his mother had thought through the funeral details. Second, knowing that all the residents of this mobile home park were elderly adults, he challenged them to plan their own funeral arrangements and record their decisions and requests.

The second illustration or scenario points to what regularly occurs when I meet with a family after their parent has died. Whenever the parents have recorded the directives, including the funeral service wishes, the children express a degree of relief as they give me a page with all the details.

However, on occasion, I see grief and a sense of helplessness coming together. To illustrate, a spouse died in the hospital. My wife Edith and I were called by the family to the bedside. With the family standing around the deceased loved one, we shared in their grief and comforted them by reading a Bible passage and praying. Following this, I asked, "Can we help make plans for the service?" I followed this with, "Have you selected a funeral home?" On this occasion, the family responded, "No, we have not selected a funeral home nor made any plans." I did not probe any further, realizing that the family had likely not thought of any other matters. They could have preplanned, as the parent had been critically ill for quite a long time. This was not the time to advise the family on the need to make prearrangements. I simply said, "Can we meet? I'll help you."

The above scenario occurs on a fairly regular basis. I need to exercise compassion and patience with families who have not made any plans, even if they have journeyed with a failing parent or spouse in palliative condition for weeks. Those experiencing grief and loss do not need the added guilt that would come from being told what they should have done.

I have known children who refused to plan a parent's funeral even though it was apparent that the parent had only days left to live. The reason they gave was, "We don't want to bury mother before she is dead." Thinking through details ahead of time is not the same as wishing the person dead. Instead, it is an act of care to express love to the deceased that will include this person's wishes.

3. Preplanning while You Still Can

There are numerous contacts to make and items to consider in making funeral arrangements. These will involve the person's family, church, business associates, and friends—and a funeral director. Then, it is important that the family knows the deceased person's decisions if those have been made. (Some of these items will be explained in greater detail in the rest of this manual.)

The following are some of the decisions that need to be made:
• Writing a life story.
• Noting special things to be included in a service.
• Selecting a speaker, musicians, and people to give tributes. These should be some of the first contacts.
• Selecting favorite Bible verses to be referred to by the pastor, to be mentioned in the service, or to be printed in a funeral bulletin.
• Determining if there will be a cremation or a burial service. (The issue of cremations versus traditional burial services will be discussed later in this book.) If it is decided to have a burial service, will there be a funeral service with the body present, or will the body be buried, followed by a memorial service?
• Selecting and making arrangements with the funeral director.

Here are two illustrations of how parents planned ahead of time for their funeral service. In the first story, the father carefully and thoughtfully considered his family. In the second, the parents planned but failed to consider how the plans would impact the children.

After the death of her spouse, a widow requested that my wife and I come to her home to meet with her and the children. In this case, the husband had written out his funeral wishes and placed them in a sealed envelope. This envelope was to be opened only after he passed away. The reason we were called to the home was that the deceased husband had requested my involvement in the funeral service. The point of this story is not my involvement but the spirit in the room of the grieving family. Certainly, there was deep grief because the husband and father had just died. But there was also a feeling of comfort and hope. The man had taken a lot of time to choose his words and write down his love to his family, and also his requests, so that his grieving family would be given hope and courage to move on without him. He had processed how his death would impact his family. He cared for them. The words, possibly written months or years earlier, helped the family when they needed comfort.

In the second illustration, the parents gave specific directives for their funerals but had not thought through how these decisions would be received by the children. It became apparent that some of the instructions were felt as insensitive by the children. The children were left having to explain to their uncles, aunts, and other people what everyone recognized were not the best instructions. Family members asked the grieving children, "Did your parents really request what you are doing?" And, since the answer was, "Yes," then the next question was, "Why did your parents want that?" This second question was usually not asked, but it lingered in the minds of the relatives and friends.

My point is simply this: please think through how your decisions will affect others. Will your decisions put your children in a dilemma? Make decisions that will help in the grieving process, not hinder it.

In the first story, the father carefully thought about how he could help, by giving hope and comfort to his grieving wife and children. Family members felt honored and respected as they opened the envelope that carried his instructions. They found it easy to carry out their father's wishes because they knew these were given out of deep love for them.

In the second story, it seemed as though the parents did not realize that their directions would make things difficult and challenging for their children. Even though the children loved their parents, it was awkward and difficult to carry out their wishes. They, along with other family members, wished that the parents had not given some of the directives.

Placing final wishes in a sealed envelope might not be your preference. Your choice might be that all such plans should be discussed with the children before the parent passes away. When parents choose to give their last wishes in a sealed envelope, my concern is that these will be given to bless and provide the surviving family members with encouragement, comfort, and directions to help in their grieving. (I agree with author Thomas G. Long that this is not controlling from beyond the grave.)

a. Respecting the Parents' Plans

Before I note specific items that parents will need to consider in planning their funeral, I want to address children on how to respond to their parents' directives and wishes regarding a funeral service.

In most funerals I have observed, children will do all they can to honor their parents, specifically regarding their parents' wishes and how they will carry out the plans for their parents' funerals.

On a few occasions, I was sad as I observed that children did not honor their parents as they planned their parents' funeral service and did not carry out their parents' spoken and written requests and directions. I have listened to the life stories of dedicated believers written by their children. I know that the parents' spiritual walk and relationship to God was a very important element of their lives. But as the children developed and read their parents' life stories, there was little or no reference to the parents' faith and to their relationship to God. I consider it disrespectful for children to ignore or minimize what is most significant to their parents. On some occasions, I have heard children callously state, "We know our father would want such and such, but he is not here. Now we will arrange the service the way we want it, not as he would want it or even how he spelled it out."

I urge readers to honor the wishes of their parents when planning a funeral service, especially when the requests are clearly written out. Even when the wishes are not spelled out, the children or those responsible for the service will usually have a good idea what their mother or father would have wanted. If children are tempted to impose their personal values and belief system and ignore their mother's or father's spirituality, the time to do so is definitely not at the parent's funeral service. I cannot say this any clearer or stronger: if one's parent or loved one gave clear

> **Giving Honor**
> In our Western culture, we tend to honor youth at the expense of giving seniors their due. However, children and grandchildren often express love and honor of their elders at funeral services. Two of the most inspiring examples of honor are when grandchildren create a pictorial life story accompanied with music that their grandparent loved, and when grandchildren express their love in singing a song that expresses the faith of their grandparent.

directions, please do all you can to carry them out. The people at a funeral service, the close friends and other family members, will recognize immediately if the children are not fulfilling the requests of their parent. Even if a child does not share the parent's values, the child should respect the parent's wishes in this, the last public and formal opportunity in which the child can honor the parent.

Another aspect of honoring a mother and father in how children plan the parent's funeral service is that these children are setting a precedent for their own children and grandchildren. When adult sons or daughters respect their elderly parent who has just passed away, their sensitivity will set an example for their children. How they respect or disrespect their parents will impact how their children will respect or disrespect them. Children who disrespect their parents are sowing seeds of disrespect in their own children.

God promises to bless children when they honor their parents. God declared this in the well-known Ten Commandments. The first command on how humans are to treat one another applies to the matter of respecting a parent's wishes. This command is, "Honor your father and your mother, so that you may live long in the land the LORD your God is giving you" (Exodus 20:12). The Apostle Paul included this command in a letter to Christians in these words: "Honor your father and mother—which is the first commandment with a promise—that it may go well with you and that you may enjoy long life on the earth" (Ephesians 6:2-3). Honoring a parent will include esteeming, caring for, showing respect for, and obeying. What better way to honor a parent than to carry out a parent's final wishes. The harsh reality is that the opposite is also true—God will not bless people who do not honor their parents.

Here I wish to give a word to the extended family and friends. When children have gone out of their way to honor their parents with thoughtful funeral arrangements, take the time to let these children know. Tell the children how the life story they prepared of their father, or the special arrangement of their mother's keepsakes, touched your heart.

But what do we say when we sense the children are not following their parent's requests? When is the right time to speak to children on this matter? Is there ever a good time to speak to other people, criticizing the children? Should this be at the funeral service, because that is when it happened and when everyone was together? My answer is a clear and definite "No." What will that accomplish? Certainly, a pastor needs to be sensitive even when he knows what the parent wished and when he realizes that the children have not followed the parent's request. This applies to friends and extended family members as well. No one knows all that has happened in a family. Words spoken during a time of loss can go deep. Therefore, I urge that we guard our words. It is problematic and complex to challenge behavior that we believe is not honoring to the deceased. On the other hand, maybe it is time that we, in our Western culture, speak up and lead the way in honoring our elders. An excellent time to do so is at funerals. The best response to those who don't honor their parents is to lead by example. When it is our responsibility to plan our parents' funerals, may we do our best in honoring our parents.

b. Dealing with Deep Hurts

Possibly, as you read these words about honoring your parents as you plan their funeral service, you feel deep hurts caused by your parents. Your mother or father hurt you to the core of your being. You have attempted to ignore the pain. But, as you stood at the bedside of your mother when she took her last breath, your mind was glued on a painful event that happened in your childhood or youth or even your adulthood. You wonder: how can I honor my parents when they have hurt me so deeply? This is certainly not an easy question. As you look in the mirror of your life, you feel your hurts. Answers don't come easily. (Dealing with deep hurts will be dealt with in more detail in Chapter Ten, "Restoring Peace in Relationships as We Near the Finish Line.")

4. Selecting a Funeral Home

As a pastor, I partner with various funeral homes. Families know that we as pastors connect with different funeral homes, and they often ask our opinion and advice on choosing one. The most critical thing I look for in a funeral director is empathy and compassion. Does the funeral director display a caring attitude? Will the family feel cared for in their time of need? These are critical questions. Therefore, if you are planning your own funeral or that of a loved one, may I suggest you ask other people who have bought services from a funeral home. Then contact one or more funeral homes and make your own assessment.

> **Things to Consider**
> The central focus of every funeral home should be a commitment to serve and meet the needs of the family. Thomas Lynch, a funeral director, stated that the function of a funeral home is to "serve the living by caring for the dead." (Thomas G. Long and Thomas Lynch, *The Good Funeral: D*, 81.) Other services a funeral home could provide include:
> • Contacting the newspaper
> • Contacting the cemetery
> • Being present at the memorial service
> • Being present at the burial
> • Being available for a viewing
> • Providing bereavement support after the service

I will first discuss the matter of making funeral prearrangements. Then I will share four stories. I definitely recommend that individuals make prearrangements and inform their family of these plans. However, I need to give a caution as these arrangements are made. In some instances, a family has reacted with disappointment and even surprise regarding the prearrangements that had been made. I remember a widow showing me the prearrangement form and the amounts that her deceased husband had paid for various items when he had "prearranged" his funeral. For each item, the amount paid covered only a fraction of the actual cost. No wonder the funeral director had made a sale. Yet, this husband had believed he had done the right thing and had provided his wife with a fully paid prearranged funeral.

Comparing funeral homes is similar to comparing apples and watermelons—not apples and oranges, but apples and watermelons. By this I mean that the contrast between funeral homes can be very great. The differences are on the critical issue of the level of compassion and on the items that are included. You will only find out about these differences as you ask thoughtful questions. A careful analysis will minimize surprises and disappointments.

The funeral director's purpose is to help a family in their time of grief. Part of this service will be providing products and services such as care of the body, cremation or embalmment, coffins or urns, bulletins, death certificates, burial plots, and flowers. But the focus needs to be on compassion. The family should never be left with any questions or confusion about what was paid for and what was not paid for.

As you process the matter of purchasing a pre-need contract, you will want to be clear about what is actually involved. The normal funeral contract provides the option to purchase a funeral package at today's price that will cover the expenses at the time of need when the costs will be considerably more. One criticism often leveled at a funeral contract is that it is simply an overpriced insurance policy. This might be the case with some prearranged plans offered by some funeral directors, but this is not the case with the funeral prearranged plans I am aware of. Here I need to stress the point that you need to be clear on all the details of the plans you are considering.

The following four experiences with funeral directors will help answer the question: "Did the family members feel cared for in the time of deepest need?" As you read these four stories you will want to ask yourself, "Which funeral director would I choose to provide the services for my funeral or that of a loved one?"

In the first story, an elderly woman had made the prearrangements for her sister's funeral service. She had also processed the funeral details and other concerns with my wife and me considerably earlier when another sister had died. Recognizing that, at her advanced age, she was unsure of her ability to make the best decisions, I suggested that she involve someone else who would help her walk through

> **Looking at Death**
> At times, an author will change society's perception about a whole industry. Jessica Mitford's book *The American Way of Death* (published in 1963 and revised in 1998) influenced conventional wisdom so that people believed "funeral directors are determined to sell you something you don't want for a price you can't afford, by preying on your grief and guilt." The result was that people began to believe only two questions were required: "How much did you spend? How much did you save?"—as if the math of caskets mattered most. (Thomas G. Long and Thomas Lynch, *The Good Funeral*, 68-69.) It is time we took another look at death, loss, and grief, not through the lens of a bank statement, but through the lens of compassion, love, caring, and relationships.

the details. In this regard, I encourage anyone who might feel overwhelmed with all the necessary responsibilities to meet with a trusted friend, family member, spiritual director, or pastor to seek help with walking through all the decisions. When the woman's sister died, she requested that I sit with her as she met with the funeral director to review the arrangements for the funeral. The funeral director expressed sympathy while she told the story. Only after she had shared her heart and grief did he open up the file and carefully go through all the items, ensuring that her wishes would be carried out and that there were no uncertainties.

> **Taking Care**
> "The son of a funeral director, who later also became a funeral director, heard his father say, 'Take care of the service and the sales will take care of themselves.' In describing all the exhibits at a convention attended by more than 1,200 funeral directors, this son described all 'such things as accessories only to the fundamental obligation to assist with the funeral. A death in the family was not a sales op, rather it was an opportunity to serve.'"
> (Thomas G. Long and Thomas Lynch, *The Good Funeral*, 24.)

In the second story, an elderly couple had also made the prearrangements. When one spouse died, the surviving spouse, together with all the children, met with the funeral director. The husband told me that the first thing the funeral director said as the grieving family had gathered in the funeral home was, "Now, what should we talk about?" The family members looked in shock at one another. They expected the funeral director to lead the conversation. They were in grief and needed the director to help with the details. It was not up to the family to process what needed to be done. The funeral director was responsible to ensure all the details were clear. Instead, he added an element of frustration and confusion to the family's grief.

In the third story, the viewing was early in the morning before the family left for the cemetery. After a specified time, the director placed the coffin in the funeral coach and began driving to the cemetery about twenty miles away. He did not give any instructions or directions to the family members who were also driving to the cemetery. Had the funeral director driven this route so often that he assumed the family knew the way as well? The result was that some of the family members could not keep up with the funeral coach and did not know the directions to the cemetery. But they knew that I, as pastor, was on my way to the cemetery and would know the direction, so they could follow me.

In the fourth story, the family requested that I sit with them as they met with the funeral director. In this case, the parents had made prearrangements and had decided on cremation. When the funeral director, who was new in the company, became aware that the family had not requested the funeral home's services at the cemetery, he said that it was up to the family to make arrangements with the cemetery. I was shocked when he said this. In actuality, he was stating that this funeral home would not provide the most basic and essential services. Since I had not been present when the family had made the prearrangements, I concluded that either those were the agreements that had been made or the funeral home had a new policy. I did not want to put a negative assessment on the funeral home in front of the family while they were experiencing deep grief in the loss of a husband and father. They did not need to be told that this funeral home was not providing even the most basic care. I assured the family I would help with this item. When I left the home, I contacted the cemetery directly and made the necessary arrangements. Later, the owner of that funeral home apologized to the family. His new employee had failed to provide some basic services, did not know the company policy, and certainly did not show compassion when it was needed.

These stories from different funeral homes illustrate that funeral directors are expected to care. I have heard many comments about funeral homes. Most are very affirming. Other comments illustrate that the expected service is not always provided. Since there is a wide variety in the options provided, I urge that people ask questions about the services that are available and that will be included in a pre-need contract.

One example of the services a funeral home provides is placing an obituary in the local newspaper. Funeral homes know the necessary procedure and can assist families in this matter. Some funeral homes provide this service at no additional cost. Other funeral homes do not provide this service, and in that case the family members will need to find out what is involved and make the arrangements themselves.

As you decide which funeral home to select, you will be considering people who will walk with you and your family through a most difficult time of life. This means you will expect these people to listen carefully to your concerns, feel your pain, and then do their best to meet your wishes. A funeral director cannot take away your grief and loss. But he or she can walk with you in your grief. I hear many stories about how funeral directors have assisted grieving families. Some directors will go out of their way to do whatever they can for the families.

As you make funeral prearrangements, speak with people who have had a recent funeral service. Take the time to visit several funeral homes and speak to the funeral directors in their premises. Choose the one which will best help you in your time of need.

5. Planning Reveals Our Core Values

This chapter has touched on the importance of planning ahead and some of the aspects that are included in our planning. We might know the components in planning a secure retirement or even the specific details involved in planning a funeral. We can place a price tag on the various parts involved. Wise planning is certainly necessary and prudent in all phases of life—including retirement and funerals. However, every decision involves more

> **Price versus Value**
> We might know the price of all the items involved in a funeral, but do we know the value of these items? Also, why do we do what we do and not do some other things?

than a price component. It involves a value behind the decision. How we spend or invest our money exposes our values—whether we are consciously aware of them or not. We will want to examine these values. Writing this book has given me an opportunity to examine my own core values. My desire is that this will be the case with you.

Reflection #1

If I am the executor for someone who has died—and therefore have the responsibility and authority to plan the funeral—what will I be more likely to do: meet with the funeral director and plan the funeral on my own or do my utmost to involve other people, especially other family members? The reality is that planning a funeral can become complicated and even messy when more people are involved. Family members might not agree on even basic issues. How will I then extend grace as I plan the funeral with other people and listen to all their wishes?

• What have I written down about my funeral plans and where are these plans kept?

• What key people have I talked to about these plans? Who else might I need to talk with?

If I am choosing to provide my final wishes in a sealed envelope, may my desire be to consider how these wishes will be heard and received by my loved ones.

Reflection #2

If I am the daughter or the son and thinking ahead about my parent's funeral service, what are some things I will want to say that will express my gratitude and honor to them?

Reflection #3

When it comes to deciding on a funeral home:

• What is keeping me from contacting a funeral home and starting to make arrangements?

• What am I waiting for?

• If I am the executor, and the funeral arrangements have not been made, how will I consider the wishes of all the family members in the various decisions?

Prayer

Heavenly Father, with Moses, I pray: teach me to number my days aright, that I may gain a heart of wisdom. I need to recognize that I will not be here forever. My days will come to an end. May I therefore be conscious of my frailty. Certainly, this applies to all the decisions I make each day, the minor ones and the significant ones. Then give me courage to plan ahead and do so with the goal that you will be given thanks and praise throughout my life. May this be evident in the planning of my funeral service. May it be evident in my life now and in my funeral that for me to live is Christ and to die is gain. In Jesus' name, Amen.

Chapter Four
Parts of a Funeral Service

1. Naming of the Service

Traditionally, a gathering to remember a departed person has been called a "funeral service." However, when the burial precedes the service, the gathering may be called a "memorial service" or, alternatively, "a celebration of life." This last designation denotes that the family is thanking God for the life and faith of their loved one. The title "memorial service" signifies that the family is inviting those attending to thank God for their memories of a person. This includes a celebration of the life and the legacy of the loved one. The choice of what to call the service is a critical issue and might also be a sensitive matter. A family will often state they wish to name the service a "celebration of life" because the members want to celebrate the life of their loved one. However, in other instances a family might be just as emphatic that the service not be called a "celebration." I remember preparing a service with a family that had experienced a lot of pain and abuse. This family could not celebrate, nor were they ready to do so. They were not only experiencing grief but also remembering painful family experiences. There was no hesitation that the service should not be called a "celebration of life."

I invite you to consider how you wish to name your service. If at all possible, ensure that all family members agree on the nature of the service, including what it will be called.

2. Viewing

As I was discussing the various aspects of the funeral service with a family, an adult daughter commented, "My children can't stomach viewing Grandma's body. Why would we have a viewing anyway?"

a. Reasons People Do Not View the Body

There are two reasons people give for why we should not view a deceased body. The first reason is this: "I want to remember the person how she or he was when she/he was strong and healthy. I want to keep those memories."

I will respond to this first reason people give for not viewing a dead body by asking two sets of questions. My first question in response is this: Will these people not visit their friend—or even their mother—after she has had a stroke and cannot speak? Will these people not visit their parent or their child after that person has suffered severe burns and the face is disfigured? I believe that in most cases these people will visit a mother who has had a major stroke or will care for a child who is disfigured with facial burns. We would agree that when we refuse to visit a person who has a major deformity, this is an expression of insensitivity that we trust is not in any of us. When a friend has suffered a stroke or another debilitating disease, this is precisely the time we will want to come alongside this friend. At such a time of need, we should be expressing our love, our grace, our acceptance, and our compassion. We cannot abandon a person just because he or she is suffering physically and is unable to respond. We don't stop loving and caring for people when there is little dignity left. And who defines dignity, and how is dignity defined?

My second question in response to this reason is: Will the people who do not want to view a deceased body not wish to be cared for when their bodies are not perfect and beautiful, but frail, dependent, and even deformed? The answer will no doubt be a definite, "They will not want to be forsaken when their bodies seem to fail them."

Funeral Viewing

Funeral homes normally have a chapel and an adjacent room where the family and friends can gather for refreshments. When there is a viewing, the body will be in the chapel and people can then visit in the next room. One funeral director made an observation that some families gather around the coffin but other families gather as far away as possible from the body.
• Does this indicate a person's comfort level with the ultimate issues of life and death?
• Do I keep my distance from the coffin?
• Why might this be?

Our Bodies are Important

"'To say that there is 'something more,' albeit unseen, is not to say that what we do see is 'something less.' The bodies of the dead are not 'just' anything or 'only' anything else….Whatever our responses to death might be…they are firstly and undeniably connected to the embodied remnant of the person who was" (Thomas G. Long and Thomas Lynch, *The Good Funeral*, 79).

The second reason some people resist having or going to a viewing is based on their theological beliefs. They state that, since the "real person" is not here anymore, no effort should be made to make the body appear pleasant or resemble how the person appeared in life. They will say, "The person—our mother, grandmother, or friend—is not here anymore. So why do we gather around the shell of a person? This is only her tent. The spirit of our mother is with Jesus—that is her real self. She is gone. She is not here."

I will respond to this reason by examining our understanding of the human body. Once we have a greater and more informed understanding of the human body, we will realize that gathering around a person's body is a natural consequence of this perception. I will begin with a Greek understanding of personhood and then go on to suggest how a society's values are measured by its treatment of a human body. Finally, I will offer a brief biblical understanding of the human body.

> **Only a Tent?**
> The Apostle Paul and the Apostle Peter described our bodies as "earthly tents" (2 Corinthians 5:1, 2 Peter 1:13). But that Jesus, the eternal Son of God, became flesh in this tent must give us a great appreciation of our "tent" (John 1:14, Philippians 2:5-11). Our body might be only a tent, but it is a phenomenal tent!

b. Understanding Personhood

i. The Greek Understanding of Personhood

Whether we realize this or not, our society is influenced by Greek philosophy, which views people in a dualistic way. This view is that human persons *have* a body. Therefore, when the body is dead, the body is of little or no consequence because the person is self-evidently separate from the body. The body is then only a shell, only a tent, that housed the real person. W. Ross Hastings argues that "we *are* an animated body, a body animated by the life or soul God has given them (not 'a body housing a soul'). After we die, when Christ returns, we will be resurrected and once again be living, integrated body-soul, whole persons" (W. Ross Hastings, *Where Do Broken Hearts Go?*, 103).

> **Understanding Viewing**
> Conscious or unconscious reasons regarding why we do or do not view the body of a deceased person:
> 1. Greek understanding of personhood.
> 2. The view a society has of personhood.
> 3. A biblical understanding of personhood.

ii. The View a Society Has of Personhood

Thomas G. Long argues convincingly that how we, as a society, treat the bodies of the dead "tells us much about what we believe about life and death, what we think of ourselves as a society. A corpse is entrusted to the care of the living for only a matter of hours or a few days, but how we carry out our responsibilities to the bodies of the dead is a strong clue as to how we will treat the bodies of the living. A culture prepared to hide the bodies of the dead as if they were an embarrassment or an insult to the living or to throw the bodies of indigent dead into a common ditch is also a society prone to cast aside its elderly, neglect its sick, leave its poor without shelter, and deprive its young of proper care" (Thomas G. Long and Thomas Lynch, *The Good Funeral*, 86-87). Long continues, "So, our deepest ethical and spiritual wisdom calls us not only to watch vigilantly over the bodies of the living but also to care tenderly for the bodies of the dead. So why don't we do it?...We are rapidly becoming the first society in the history of the world for whom the dead are no longer required—or desired—at their own funerals" (93).

Here I wish to make a comment about the presence of a coffin in a service. A generation or two ago, nearly every service was a funeral service with the body present. Currently, very few services have the body present. Has this shift been biblically and theologically driven? Are we embarrassed to have an open coffin before a service? We will normally close it during a funeral service, but what are the reasons for the shift in practice and for the present reluctance to have the body present in a service?

Before I briefly note that a biblical understanding of personhood will inform our treatment of the body, it is important to recognize that the major religious traditions will agree on this thesis: "We will learn wisdom about how to live when we care lovingly and reverently for the bodies of the dead." After presenting this thesis, Thomas G. Long gives four examples that demonstrate the common value of caring for the dead:

> **The Example of Tobit**
> Tobit wrote, "I buried, when I saw them, the bodies of my countrymen thrown over the walls of Nineveh. I also buried those who were killed by Sennacherib (for when he retreated from Judaea in disorder, after the King of heaven had punished his blasphemes, in his anger Sennacherib killed a great number of Israelites). So I stole their bodies to bury them; Sennacherib looked for them and could not find them." Tobit also recorded how he dug a grave and buried one of his people who was murdered, even though there was a price on Tobit's head for doing this earlier.(Tobit 1:17-20, 2:1-8, The Jerusalem Bible).

1. A very extensive search was made for the bodies of the people killed at Ground Zero on September 11, 2001, resulting in the final tally of 4,257 human remains.

2. Following the devastating Japanese tsunami of 2011, a retired undertaker, Atsushi Chiba, a Buddhist, attended to more than one thousand tsunami victims.

3. Tobit, a Jewish exile in Nineveh, got into serious trouble with the Assyrian authorities by giving the bodies of the dead a decent burial. Might I say that Tobit was in grave trouble for carefully placing people in a grave? Centuries earlier, Joseph gave instructions about his bones (Genesis 50:25).

4. The early Christians perplexed their Roman neighbors, who believed the body was merely a corrupted vessel, by taking on the role of undertaker, not just for the bodies of their own people but also for the bodies of impoverished Romans who otherwise would have been unceremoniously dumped into a common pit (Thomas G. Long and Thomas Lynch, *The Good Funeral*, 77, 88-91).

iii. A Biblical Understanding of Personhood

The first indication that the human body is precious is given in the creation story. In the creation account, a closing comment on the things that were created each day was, "And God saw that it was good." However, after God's creation of man and woman, we read, "God saw all that he had made, and it was very good" (Genesis 1:4, 10, 12, 18, 21, 25, 31). May I add that there can be no disagreement that God's comment about the essence of man and woman applied to the body as well as to the person's spirit.

God's assessment of his creation of human beings is certainly evident in a maternity unit in a hospital. When a mother and father see their newborn infant for the first time, they marvel at their child's beauty and how the child is designed in such a phenomenal manner. The Psalmist did not have the benefit of more recent medical and scientific studies to know how intricate the human body is, but, based on what he observed, he declared that the body is "fearfully and wonderfully made" (Psalm 139:14).

The second significant indication that the human body is precious is the undeniable miracle celebrated at Christmas time—"The Word became flesh and made his dwelling among us. We have seen his glory, the glory of the One and Only, who came from the Father, full of grace and truth" (John 1:14). The Apostle Paul declared the miracle of God taking on a human body in what is believed to be an early Christian hymn: "Who, being in very nature God, did not consider equality with God something to be grasped, but made himself nothing, taking the very nature of a servant; being made in human likeness" (Philippians 2:6, 7). If the eternal Son of

God, Jesus, God himself, took on the very nature of a person, this should settle the matter of the value of our human body.

We will agree that our bodies are beautiful. Certainly, we care for our bodies. This becomes obvious when we recognize the extraordinary care given in a burn unit of our hospitals or observe the delicate surgery required to restore a fractured and deformed face following a major accident. But does the beauty and magnificence of our bodies remain with them even after we have died? Furthermore, is there justification for all the effort a mortician takes to restore a face and make it appear beautiful and similar to the features a person had in life? This leads us back to the underlying question, "Why do we view the body of a deceased person?"

An excellent place to begin is by considering how people in the major religions treat the bodies of their people.

Even though the Hebrews had strict taboos regarding the human corpse and taught that a person became unclean through physical contact with a deceased person (Leviticus 21:11, 19:11-22), they still treated the body of a dead person with great respect. It was customary for someone in the immediate family to close the eyes of a departed parent, as Joseph carefully did for his father, Jacob (Genesis 46:4). The Hebrews washed the dead body (Acts 9:37), draped a napkin over the dead person's face (John 11:44), anointed the departed loved one with aromatic spices and wrapped him or her in linen materials.

> ### Respect for the Deceased
> There is a common element in major civilizations and religions in that people treat the bodies of the deceased with respect. But how the body will be treated will vary from religion to religion. Traditional Judaism rejects viewings as a person cannot and should not comfort the mourners while the dead lie before them. According to Islamic law, the body should be buried as soon after death as possible, and therefore there is no viewing. In Hinduism, viewings are allowed and usually take place before the cremation. In Buddhism, the deceased is washed and dressed in everyday clothes. Most Christian denominations allow the body to be embalmed and then viewed by loved ones. These examples from five major religions demonstrate that the body of the deceased is always treated with dignity and respect. How this is done is in keeping with the theology or beliefs of each religion. Therefore, the growing trend within Christian culture that avoids the presence of the body as an embarrassment should give us reason to pause and question our core beliefs.

An ultimate expression of treating the body of a dead person with utmost respect is noted in how people treated Jesus' body after he died. The Gospel writers describe in detail the tender care given to the body of Jesus by Joseph of Arimathea and Nicodemus. Then the writers mention the love shown by the women who purchased and prepared spices to give further care to Jesus' body. The Gospel writers stress the importance of these acts by naming the two men as well as the women involved: Mary Magdalene, Mary the mother of Jesus, Mary the mother of James, and Salome (Matthew 27:57-61, 28:1, Mark 15:40-16:3, Luke 23:50-24:3, John 19:38-20:1).

> The Bible recognized the people by name who cared for Jesus' body, as well as the expense of the materials for caring for his body. Should this not give us pause when we minimize the people who care for the bodies of our loved ones and we attempt to spend as little as possible for their care?

One principle we use to develop our interpretation of a theme or topic in the Bible is to note how many times this topic is mentioned in the Bible. When a topic is mentioned numerous times by various biblical authors throughout the Bible, then we can draw the conclusion that this is a biblical truth we need to recognize as significant. On this basis, it is noteworthy that each of the four Gospel writers mentioned the people who cared for Jesus' body by name. May we follow this example as we consider the value we place on bodies once a person is dead.

The following words point to the respect and care we need to give to a body: "Caring attentiveness to the 'mortal remains' is a token of care and respect both for the one who has died and for those who grieve. The person is dead, the body

How They Treated Jesus
In the Gospels, we notice how Jesus' enemies devalued and degraded Jesus and how his friends valued him. Judas, who betrayed Jesus, accepted the extremely low assessment that was given to Jesus by the religious leaders, that of an injured slave—30 pieces of silver, a trifling amount (Exodus 21:32, Zechariah 11:12, Matthew 26:14-16). The Roman soldiers stripped the clothing off Jesus and gambled for his inner garments, thereby giving the lowest possible value to Jesus. In contrast, Mary spent the equivalent of a year's wages to purchase perfume to anoint Jesus for his burial (Matthew 26:6-13, John 12:1-8). Then, Nicodemus paid an extravagant price to purchase seventy-five pounds of myrrh and aloes to anoint Jesus' body, and Joseph of Arimathea gave his own tomb (John 19:38-42).

will decay; relationships are broken; communities are dismembered. But the body was once—and still is—identified with the person who had died. The body was once—and still is—the medium by which we display the affection, loyalty, and honor due the person" (Allen Verhey, *The Christian Art of Dying*, 254).

It appears that viewing is becoming less common in our Western culture. The practice of viewing varies between subgroups, seeming to be more frequent in rural, conservative settings than in urban settings. A related practice that is also becoming less common is for the community to gather at a graveside service.

c. Reasons to View the Body of the Deceased

If viewing is becoming less common, we need to consider a primary question seriously: "Why do we gather at a funeral home, a church, or even a home to view a dead person?" I suggest several reasons why it is a good idea to view the body of the deceased. These reasons are not given in any order of importance.

i. Accept the Reality of Death

By viewing the body of the deceased, we accept the fact that this person has died. The presence of the body emphasizes that the person has died. It establishes the fact of death.

ii. Honor and Express Gratitude

We gather to honor and express our gratitude to the person who has meant so much to us. We pause, reflecting on the impact this person has made in our lives.

> **Reasons to View the Body**
> • Accept the reality of death
> • Honur and express gratitude
> • Remember
> • Take up the torch
> • Support each other
> • Express our trust in God in our grief
> • Step out of a room without the loved one
> • Proclaim our hope
> • Offer a final thanksgiving for this gift of life

At the funeral home, the coffin is placed in the front of the chapel, allowing people to come quietly to the coffin and reflect. If the funeral home does not have a chapel, I suggest that the coffin be placed at the front of a sanctuary. Some individuals will visit in the foyer while other people will pray and solemnly and quietly reflect on the loved one whose body is in the coffin. In some traditions, the body will be placed in a large room in the house of the deceased. Friends and family will gather to give their respect to the person.

iii. Remember

We gather to remember special moments, some painful, and many pleasant and joyful. We gather to share these memories with an intimate circle of family and close friends. I will never forget the viewing of my mother, with our daughter holding her grandpa's hand. Then, various family members stood, quietly sharing memories about Grandma. Nothing can replace the impact of gathering around a grandmother, grandfather, wife, or husband and sharing memories. We live in a culture of mostly shallow communication where we text and communicate with many people, many of whom we hardly know. And we will likely forget almost everything we text or see on Facebook. But we will never forget the emotional sharing of an uncle or a brother as we gather around a dear mother. Also, we will never forget our own words, spoken from the depth of our heart, spoken in love and gratitude. Yes, grandmother might not hear us. But our cousins and all our family will know how much we loved our grandmother or mother.

We are familiar with the fifth commandment: "Honor your father and your mother." When I observe families gathering at the coffin of a grandmother or grandfather, I come to this deep conviction: "Here is a family that is honoring its elderly parent. Here is a family that honors and cherishes one another. And God will bless this family in return."

iv. Take Up the Torch

Here I think of the metaphor of a relay race, where one runner passes the torch or baton on to the next runner. When a family gathers around the coffin of a dear grandmother, there is a sense that the family members and friends are saying, "Mother, we thank God for your legacy. We are committed to take up the torch and lift high the godly legacy you have given us." I believe that when a son or a daughter (or a friend) walks into a quiet sanctuary to view the coffin of his or her mother, he or she is often recommitting himself or herself to God and saying, "I thank God for you, Mother. I want to be like you."

v. Support Each Other

When we gather at a viewing, we are supporting one another in our grief and loss. We live in a culture that attempts to minimize pain and grief. The Apostle Paul wrote, "Rejoice with those who rejoice" but also wrote the next line, "Weep with those who weep" (Romans 12:15).

vi. Express Our Trust in God in Our Grief

When we are at a viewing, we express our trust in a compassionate God who is present in our loss. The Psalmist David wrote many more lament psalms than praise psalms. As I study the Psalms, I do not believe the worshiper's grief was immediately removed when he poured out his soul to God. I see instead a person's confidence in God. I see a person who believed God would be there in the deepest and darkest valley.

When we quote the line, "Even though I walk through the valley of the shadow of death, I will fear no evil, for you are with me; your rod and your staff, they comfort me" (Psalm 23:4), we reassure ourselves that the Lord is with us in our grief and loss. We do not have any guarantee that the Lord will immediately take us out of the "valley of the shadow of death," but we are assured that he is with us and will comfort us in the valley of death.

As I read the story of Jesus at the graveside of his friend Lazarus, I notice seven references to Jesus' deep emotions, particularly grief (John 11). Throughout Jesus' time of grief over the death of his friend, Jesus responded to Martha's and Mary's concerns and emotions with the utmost sensitivity and compassion. Another aspect to note is that even though Jesus knew he would perform the miracle of raising Lazarus to life within a few minutes, he felt the deep grief and loss that Lazarus had died.

> **Jesus' Emotions at His Friend's Death (John 11)**
> 1. Jesus was concerned about Mary and asked to see her.
> 2. Jesus saw Mary weeping.
> 3. Jesus was deeply moved in spirit and troubled.
> 4. Jesus showed concern by asking, "Where have you laid him?"
> 5. Jesus wept.
> 6. The Jews said, "See how Jesus loved Lazarus."
> 7. Jesus, once more deeply moved, came to the tomb.

Christianity does not shrink back from death. It does not force a smile to mask our grieving. Our sadness because of the loss of a dear one should be obvious. We cannot cover up grief, even though we may attempt to do so. We must come alongside one another, embracing each other in our grief. It is never appropriate to denigrate, minimize, or ignore the grieving process. Our belief in Jesus who is "the resurrection and the life" does not shield us from feeling loss when death occurs. We have heard the saying, "A grief shared is half a grief," but it is still a grief.

We cannot hold back our grief. Nor can we forsake one another in our grief. We must come to a viewing to "weep with those who weep." We must carry each other's burdens.

vii. Stepping Out of a Room without the Loved One

This reason includes all the above reasons. Some people describe this as "bringing closure." As I stood in front of the coffin of my mother with my father, my wife, and my family, I expressed a final "Goodbye." Yes, I thanked God for all that she meant to me. Yes, I was taking up the torch she had handed me throughout my life. Yes, I was supported by a loving family. But I was in deep grief because I knew this was the final time I would see her. From that time on, I could recall memories, but I could not make any more memories. Viewing was an important part of "bringing closure." However, I will qualify the phrase "bring closure" to note that I will never bring closure to grief, as some people seem to think is possible.

> **Closure**
> What some call "bringing closure" I prefer to see as stepping out of one room and stepping into another. In the one room is the loss that I grieve. At times, I will return to this room. But I am choosing to open a door into a new room, one without the loved one.

Viewing is necessary so that we can be released to move along in our grief and on to the next phase, a difficult phase which will not include our loved one. When I use the phrase, "move through our grief," I do not mean we will ever move completely out of grief. There will always be moments when we will be reminded of our loved ones, possibly at significant times of the year such as Christmas, birthdays, and anniversaries. What I mean is that we choose to move "through our grief" and not attempt to avoid it and think we can move around it.

Viewing is one aspect of closing a door so that I can open another door, stepping out of the room where my loved one remains behind and stepping into a room without a loved one. This is necessary.

viii. Proclaim Our Hope

This is the supreme principle that supports viewing. How I wish that over every coffin with a loved one's body were the words, "We Preach Christ Crucified and Risen" (1 Corinthians 15), the church motto on the wall at the front of our church sanctuary. How I wish over every coffin was a cross and a picture of an open grave.

• We gather to bow before the cross of Jesus, whose blood secured our salvation and the salvation of our loved one.
• We gather to celebrate that our loved one is alive because Jesus rose from the dead.
• We gather in grief, knowing that we will not see our loved one again here on earth.
• We gather in hope, knowing that we will see our loved one with Jesus in heaven.
• We gather in hope, knowing that Christ was crucified and Christ rose from the dead.

ix. A Final Thanksgiving for the Gift of this Life

This final reason for viewing leads into an element that is often part of a viewing—a brief meditation and a prayer. A family might request that a pastor share some Bible verses and pray. Or the family might select one of its own members to bring their hearts together under God. This will usually be a short meditation but yet a distinct word in which the family is stating, "Mother's life revolved around God. When we gather for the last time with her, we will focus on God as well as our mother."

3. Flowers

Flowers are a visual expression of our love, both for the deceased and for the family that remains behind.

Some people insist, "Why provide flowers that will perish in several days?" This argument has little validity. Should a husband excuse never giving flowers to his wife, even on their anniversary or her birthday, with the argument, "Why should I give her flowers that will perish and wilt in several days?"

Some people even assert, "Why spend money for flowers that are in memory of a person who is not able to appreciate them?" Flowers are certainly for the living, an expression of our love and support. These flowers also express our love for the dead. The flowers show how much the loved one meant to us.

This relates to the caring practice of placing flowers at the graveside of our loved one. This can be done on the anniversary of a death, on an occasion such as the birthday of the loved one, Mother's Day, or Father's Day, or whenever the family can be together.

In some cultures, the giving of flowers is a daily and regular practice that is far more prominent than for many people in our Western culture. A husband will sometimes pick up a bouquet on his way home just to express his love for his wife. He will not wait until her birthday or their anniversary. I believe we need to express our love on a regular basis and in a tangible manner. Thus, the giving of flowers at a funeral will be a natural expression of our love.

4. Donations in Memory of a Loved One

As noted above, I believe flowers should be plentiful at a funeral service. However, my viewpoint is that donations should never replace flowers—nor should flowers replace donations. I suggest that when a family is choosing to encourage people to give donations in memory of their loved one, these words be used: "Donations in memory of (name of loved one) may be given for the (name of specific ministry)."

I realize that some families do not want to highlight any specific foundation, agency, or ministry. Their loved one might have given regular contributions to a particular ministry or agency. However, the family might not choose to invite people to give to this ministry but will say instead, "Please give a donation to the agency or ministry of your choice."

I take another approach. I believe that a funeral service is an appropriate and natural setting to highlight a ministry or mission that a beloved mother believed in and supported. I will be so bold as to encourage the family to donate towards the specific ministry that their mother supported. It is good if they set the example that other people will follow.

When you select an agency or ministry, you will want to ensure this is a government-registered charity in the event that people wish to receive a donation receipt for their gift.

5. Obituary/Eulogy/Life Story/Tributes

First, we need to be clear regarding the differences between the various written or spoken items about the loved one.

a. The Obituary

An obituary is a short account of a person's life that includes key events. This is the brief write-up that will be published in a local newspaper. Such a summary informs the community that a person has passed away. A family might choose to place two notices in the paper, first a brief notice that their loved one has died and then a longer notice giving the details of the time and place of the funeral service.

b. A Life Story or Eulogy

The word, "eulogy," is a compound word consisting of "*eu*" meaning "well, good" and "*logos*" meaning "word." In other words, it is a "good word" about a loved family member or friend. I use "eulogy" and "life story" interchangeably. A life story begins with the basic facts that comprise an obituary. Then, various elements are expanded, and personal reflections and memories are added.

We all have a story. A funeral service provides an opportunity to write and then share our story. But our story is much more than "a string of biographical facts." I strongly encourage each of us write our own story. We have the opportunity to write how we wish to be remembered.

There are several questions regarding our eulogy or life story:
• Who will write our story?
• What is the purpose of our story?
• What do we want included in our written legacy?

If we neglect to record our story when we can choose what to include and still have clarity of mind, then our children will need to compose our story. Normally, children will wait until we have passed away. At that time, they will need to take care of many other funeral details and therefore will have limited time to write our story. They will also be grieving their loss. Further, if we have several children, would we prefer that one child over the other children write our story? That choice will not be ours once we are gone.

The normal practice is to write a brief story that is limited to the basic details. However, when it comes to a written life story that will be available at a funeral, I encourage individuals to take a different perspective on their life stories than what is normally the pattern. I urge this whether an individual is writing his or her own story or the children are writing the life story of a parent. Some families state that there is no purpose in having a written life story if it will be read in the service. My response is that this will give the family an ideal opportunity to provide a written legacy of their loved one, one that will be read and reread and cherished by friends and certainly by family members.

A life story might be compared to a will. In a will, a person directs a legal distribution of her/his material possessions. In a life story, a person has the opportunity to share about another part of her or his life. This is the person's spiritual and personal legacy. In a life story, a mother can leave her spiritual legacy by noting how God met and called her, listing specific landmarks on her faith journey, citing Bible verses that were special to her, and describing her relationship with God. We will never fully know how our lives impact our children and grandchildren and friends, but in our life story we can share, "This is how Jesus called me to himself. This is why I love Jesus. This is part of my journey with a faithful and forgiving God."

We return to the question, "What if the person has not written a life story?" This provides the family with an opportunity to honor their loved one. As family members write the life story of their mother, they will have a wonderful privilege to express their love. They will be able to let the other family members and their friends know who their mother really was.

I remember one family that initially saw little significance in preparing and providing a written life story. However, after I invited the members to realize the value of having a lasting written legacy, this family became inspired and committed to write the best possible life story of their mother. Their intention was to have the eulogy available for distribution at the memorial service. But the family member responsible for writing the life story kept making revisions and adding new things until late into the night before the memorial service. There were so many significant pieces the daughter wanted to include. Even though this family was unable to provide a printed life story at the time of the funeral, they later made a printed copy available to anyone who requested one.

Take the time to show your love for your mother. Your children and other family members will learn things they never knew about their grandmother. They will thank you and cherish every word, especially when you include photos with the story that show how much your mother loved her family. In our church, we gladly assist with printing the story that shows a family's love for a dear mother. Regularly, a family member, often a granddaughter, will create a thoughtful printed life story with beautiful photos. You will not be sorry you took the extra time.

c. Tributes

In addition to an obituary and a eulogy, there will often be tributes in a funeral service. A tribute consists of words of appreciation for the life and the achievements of a person. The purpose of a tribute is to share specific memories and express how the loved one left a positive impact on the speaker's life. Here I will make two suggestions that apply both to a life story and the words of tribute.

First, often every child and grandchild will want to give a personal, even a lengthy tribute. Therefore, when there are many children, with a large extended family, one recommendation is that one child speak for all her/his siblings and one grandchild speak for all the grandchildren. This also applies to the great-grandchildren. If every child and every grandchild share memories, the service can become very lengthy.

Second, some families choose to give shorter tributes during the formal funeral service and then provide the opportunity for any member of the extended family to share following the luncheon in a more informal setting.

Having given these two suggestions, I will emphasize that each family will want to do what will best express their love to the deceased in their own way. What if either the tributes given in the memorial service or the memories shared in the more informal setting become what some people will deem very lengthy? My response is that this is the only time the family is gathered to share memories at their loved one's funeral service. Do what is right and loving for you. Don't worry about what other people think regarding the length of the life story. Take all the time you need.

d. A Pictorial Life Story or a Video

Another component in many funeral services is a pictorial life story. This will include pictures of the person from birth to the final days. Whoever creates this pictorial life story should consider that this is part of the funeral service. This means the audience is not

> **Pictorial Life Story/Video**
> • Enjoy; be creative.
> • Remember the audience.
> • Label photos; not everyone knows everyone.

the same as that in an intimate family setting where everyone wants to have as many pictures as possible about themselves. I recommend that a pictorial life story not be longer than seven minutes. It is helpful to have section headings that indicate the next parts of the life to be shown. A family might select hymns or songs that their mother or father appreciated to accompany the pictures.

Some families are able to express their love for their loved one with a video. This video can be a stringing together of very short videos. Or the family might create a video just for the funeral service.

6. Children

Do we unnecessarily keep children from experiencing the loss of a grandparent or other loved one? Children have watched as a family pet, a cat or a bird, has died, or they will at least have been told the sad news that their favorite pet has died. On these occasions, we comfort our children in their grief and permit them to grieve. We take little children and show them newborn babies and want them to share our joy with them. Yet, we may hesitate to let children see the lifeless body of their grandmother, sense our deep sorrow, and reflect how this might impact them. However, as children observe the death of their grandmother and know their grandmother will never again be there for them, they must be conscious of our love and support. They must feel that we are walking with them through their own valley of the shadow of death. They might not be able to explain what they are sensing and feeling, but our desire should be that our children will experience God's love and compassion through us, their parents and their uncles and aunts in their grief.

I wish to include a testimony of a close friend who emphasized the importance of letting children be exposed to the passing of a parent. His son-in-law was only seven when his mother died of cancer. His father wanted to protect the children emotionally, and so they were not allowed to visit their mother in the hospital, nor were they allowed to attend the funeral of their mother. This had a profound effect on this man. He mentioned to his father-in-law that he would like to see his mother's grave. So, this man took his son-in-law and his wife to the cemetery. This was this son-in-law's first real opportunity to deal with his mother's death. This man hugged his father-in-law and wept for probably ten minutes and would not let go of his father-in-law. This was a very therapeutic occasion after holding his grief inside for more than forty years.

7. Bulletins

A memorial bulletin is an opportunity for the family to express affection for their loved one. A key item is the eulogy or life story. Take as much space as you wish to honor your loved one. Friends will value a printed family tree that includes children and grandchildren. If there was a special poem or a favorite Bible verse, include it. The bulletin is a short, well-defined legacy that family and friends can take home. List all the pallbearers in the bulletin. The pallbearers will then realize it is a privilege to serve and an honor to be recognized.

It is also appropriate to include a note of thanks for the love and the support expressed, an invitation to a luncheon, and an explanation regarding giving donations in memory of the loved one if this is desired.

8. Hymns, Spiritual Songs, and Special Music

As individuals prepare the various items for their memorial service, I encourage them to leave a list of the songs they want sung at their funeral service. When individuals have been blessed by special musicians, it is a good idea to write down the names of these musicians, along with the songs they request will be sung. When a funeral has been preplanned, the family and those officiating will want to honor these wishes and follow these requests. When a hymn is unfamiliar, those leading the service should make every effort to ensure the requested song is sung or at least heard or printed. The key consideration is that we do our best to follow the request of the person and not replace it with another song that is our own favorite. When no preselection of hymns has been made, those planning the service will want to select hymns that express the faith in God of the person whose service it is, at least to the best of their knowledge.

Hymns should express confidence and trust in God, acknowledge that our God is faithful, and be a witness to the hope we have in God. Our faith is rooted in a powerful and loving God who is with us now and who desires a relationship with us, his creation and his redeemed people, forever. Our faith has a future in a glorious union with our Creator and Savior.

Hymns and songs are an excellent way to remind ourselves of these truths. When we feel deep grief and possibly feel deserted and forgotten by God, hearing the old, familiar hymns is comforting because they remind us of the core truths concerning our faith in God. They acknowledge that our faith is based on a sovereign but also compassionate God. He is Lord of today, when we feel grief, but also of tomorrow, when we will be with Jesus, our Savior and our Creator. Today we can sing, "What a friend we have in Jesus." But we can also rejoice because, "There is coming a day when my Jesus I shall see." Let us never hesitate to sing songs of our faith.

When there is a soloist or a special group singing, this should not be presented as a performance in a concert. The purpose of the special music is the same as that of the songs sung by the congregation—to remind all present of our God and to express the faith and emotions of all the people in the service.

Reflection #1: Naming of the Service
   What name do I want for my service?
• A funeral?
• A memorial service?
• A celebration of life?
Have I talked with my family about what I will name the service?

Reflection #2: Viewing
How do I feel about stopping in front of the body of a dead person? Why do I think I feel this way?

Reflection #3: Life Story
• What were some key times I sensed God's faithfulness in my life?
• If I am responsible for writinge the life story of my mother or father, what special qualities will I highlight? How do I wish that other people will remember him or her?
• When I begin reflecting on my life story, I might see this as an opportunity to take stock of where I am on my spiritual journey. What were the special times when God spoke to me and I renewed my commitment to God?
• Is God bringing to my mind relationships that need mending, phone calls that need to be made?

Prayer
Heavenly Father, with the Psalmist, I declare, "I praise you because I am fearfully and wonderfully made, your works are wonderful. I know that full well." May I respond as the Psalmist did, with praise and worship of you, my Creator. When I solemnly stand by the body of a loved one, may this draw me to you for how you have designed and created, sustained and provisioned my loved one. You have created me and everyone in a wonderful way. I give you praise. May I also treat all people with utmost respect and honor, knowing you have created all human beings. I thank you for providing me with this body, knowing there is coming a glorious day when it will be transformed to be like that of your beloved Son. In Jesus' name, Amen.

Chapter Five
Burial Service, Interment, or Committal Service

1. Parts of a Burial Service

As the term "committal service" implies, in a burial service, the body or the ashes are committed to the ground. But a Christian burial service has another, more sacred meaning of committal. We are committing or giving our loved one to our heavenly Father.

As a pastor, I will begin a burial service with a few selected words of comfort for the family. Then I focus on the hope that we who believe in Jesus have by reading Bible passages. The following verses include words of comfort appropriate for a burial service:

• 2 Corinthians 1:3: God is the Father of compassion and the God of all comfort.
• John 11:25, 26: Jesus said, "I am the resurrection and the life."
• John 14:1-6: Jesus promised that he is preparing a home for us.
• 1 Corinthians 15: Jesus' resurrection is the basis for our eternal life.
• 1 Thessalonians 4:13-18: We have the promise that Jesus will return to receive us so that "we will be with the Lord forever."
• Revelation 21:1-4, 22:1-7: We have a beautiful, eternal home in heaven.

Then the service will conclude with words of committal and a prayer.

2. Coffins

A question that is asked, if not implied, is, "Why spend money on an elaborate coffin? In fact, why bother with a coffin at all?"

The selection of a coffin, as with many other aspects of a funeral, can be approached in several ways. Often the first and most common approach is that of cost. I encourage us to look at the various parts of a funeral using other criteria than only the cost.

On some occasions, a family member, usually an elderly person who has no immediate family nearby, will request my presence when meeting with the funeral director. The topic of cremation or burial will be discussed. If the choice is made for a burial, then the next question is the type and cost of a coffin. As a pastor, my goal is to listen to the heart of the person who needs to make major decisions. Certainly, the cost is a factor. The funeral director will detail the various features of a coffin. However, there are other aspects that cannot be measured by dollars, as will be evident in the following scenarios:

• Will a grandson ever forget the time he stood between two cousins carrying the coffin of his dear grandmother?
• Will a widow ever forget the moment she placed her hand on the coffin of her husband, saying, "I love you. We'll meet again"?
• Will a granddaughter ever forget when she stood with a loving family watching her grandmother being lowered into the ground?

3. Pallbearers

There is something personal and profound that happens when a son, daughter, grandson, granddaughter, or close friend carries the coffin of a loved one. In our Western society, we have delegated most of the care of a dead body to professionals such as the mortician who cleans and prepares the body, the funeral director who makes all the arrangements, and the cemetery workers who dig the grave and then close the grave after the coffin is lowered. Then, sometime later, the family will contact a company to design and make a permanent grave marker.

This means that the only nonprofessional persons who have a direct responsibility in caring for the body are the pallbearers. They have the final honor and responsibility in the care of their loved one. The pallbearers are usually selected from among the family members for this honor. Whenever I stand with pallbearers, waiting for the final instructions from the funeral director, I sense that they feel it is a special honor and privilege to carry their loved one.

When the family has chosen cremation, I observe how carefully a child, usually the oldest, will carry the urn with the ashes of a beloved mother or grandmother. As this mother has cared for her children, often carrying them when they were tired and gently placing them in their beds, now the daughter or son has the privilege and responsibility of carrying the mother and then gently placing her ashes in her final resting place.

The decision will need to be made as to who will carry the urn and place it in the prepared hole in the cemetery. There are three options: the funeral director, who is actually then an undertaker; the pastor; or a family member. It is important that this issue be decided ahead of time. I have participated in different burial services using all three options, and there is value in each.

My preference is to invite a family member, on behalf of the family, to carry the loved one and gently place the remains to rest. This can happen in one of two ways. First, with the goal of saving money, the family will pick up the urn from the funeral home. Then, the family will take the urn to the cemetery and set it beside the hole in the ground. After words of committal and prayer, the family member will lower the urn into the hole. With this option, the pastor needs to be certain as to the exact location of the burial site. I will admit that I don't favor this first way. I prefer the second option in which the funeral director acts as a genuine "undertaker" and takes care of the details, such as leading the mourners and the pastor to the exact place in the cemetery. The urn might be given to a designated family member who will lead the family to the burial site, or the funeral director will carry the urn and place it beside the designated hole. After the words of committal and prayer, the funeral director will remove the covering, the designated family member will place the urn in the hole, and then the funeral director will replace the covering.

It is important that the names of all the pallbearers are in the bulletin. If there are more than six people whom the family desires to be pallbearers and who can all equally serve as pallbearers, one approach is to select six individuals who will carry the coffin and then have the other people walk immediately behind the coffin. The goal is to include as many people as possible or as many as the family wants. Make sure that all parts of the family are represented in the selection of pallbearers. By this I mean that if there are eight children, ensure that all children are pallbearers or, if the next generation is chosen, that each family be represented.

If, on the other hand, a family has a very small group of people who can serve as pallbearers, the pastor and funeral director will assure them that other people will be available to help. Here, as in other aspects of the funeral arrangements, the funeral director, together with the pastor, will do everything necessary to ensure a family's wishes are met.

Some families will ask elderly folks, perhaps siblings or close friends, to serve as honorary pallbearers. They will walk behind the casket and in front of the family as they are able. This is especially true for burial services for military veterans.

4. Special Items in a Burial Service

Families might add items that will make the burial service special for them. As I meet with a family, I will be sensitive to their requests and also encourage the family to show their compassion for their loved one in whatever manner they choose. Also, a pastor should speak to a family about the flow of the burial service and be clear on what will happen next. In the following directions, wherever reference is made to a coffin, the practice can apply to cremation and an urn, with some necessary adjustments and modifications. These special additions to a burial service might include:

a. Placing Flowers on a Coffin

These flowers represent a special but final interaction in the relationship between the family members and their loved one in the coffin. When family members place flowers on a coffin and then observe the coffin with their flowers lowered into the ground, there is a final but loving sense of farewell and a visible act of compassion. What better way to say, "Goodbye, until we meet again in heaven," than with a rose, a symbol of love?

b. Taking Flowers from a Coffin Spray

Taking flowers from the coffin spray and giving one flower to each family member and friend at the burial service is a thoughtful way to have each person take something home to remember their loved one by.

c. Releasing Balloons

As these balloons fly into the sky, the family reflects on how the spirit of their loved one has gone up to God. Even more, the family members are looking forward to the time when they "who are still alive and are left will be caught up together with them in the clouds to meet the Lord in the air. And so we will be with the Lord forever" (1 Thessalonians 4:17).

d. Releasing Homing Pigeons

As the pigeons are released and begin their flight "home," the family is given an unmistakable and positive illustration that the spirit of their loved one has flown "home" to be with Jesus.

e. Singing a Hymn or a Spiritual Song

A family will be drawn together, remembering their loved mother and grandmother, as the family members sing a song that was their loved one's favorite. I recommend that the words of the hymn be printed and distributed so that everyone has the words. On several occasions, a child has suggested that a song be sung and then he or another person has begun singing, but the song has faltered after the first two lines because very few people knew the words. Also, some of the children and grandchildren might not be familiar with the selected hymn or favorite song. These family members might feel left out if they cannot sing with the rest of the family. Another comment about singing as a family at the graveside: the key issue is what's in your heart, not how you sound. Yet, it is wise to have a person with a strong voice lead the singing.

f. Writing Personal Words on the Coffin

One family had selected a coffin made of light-colored wood. Every family member was given a marker with which final love notes were written about and to the loved one. As I observed this moment, I sensed the family members bonded together as they lovingly wrote about their dear loved one. Yes, the written notes were buried with the coffin, but the memories will remain engraved on the hearts of those who wrote the notes and shared the moment.

g. Covering the Coffin with Dirt

In some church traditions, this is practiced more frequently than in other church traditions. I remember several times when shovels were available and the children of the person in the coffin and also other adults would begin carefully placing dirt on the coffin. I recall a daughter state, as her siblings and other adults began pouring dirt on her mother's coffin, "Mother always covered us so tenderly with a blanket each night. Now we want to cover her as well."

Regarding the matter of covering the coffin with dirt, some funeral directors will assure the family that their beloved's coffin will be taken care of by the cemetery workers as soon as the family leaves. It is not unusual to have the cemetery workers stand just off to the side of the graveside. They are there in the event that they are needed but also to assure the family that they will take care of the next details and cover the coffin.

h. Playing a Trumpet

At either the beginning or the conclusion of a burial service, a person might play the tune of a familiar song on a trumpet. Family members will never forget hearing the trumpet play the song, "When the trumpet of the Lord shall sound, and time shall be no more," as the coffin is lowered into the grave. Those words give the assurance that, even though Mother's body will remain in the grave, Jesus will call her home to be with him. The notes of the trumpet will keep ringing in the hearts of the children, giving assurance of their mother's homegoing and their own eventual homegoing as well. If the cemetery has a small hill, an idea is to have the trumpet player stand on top of the hill.

i. Sharing Memories

Realizing that the family will never gather in this way again, at the grave of this dear loved one, means that the moment is special. Individuals will naturally reflect on their relationship with the person whose body or ashes are laid to rest. Individuals will share memories. One question is whether the sharing will be structured or informal. In a structured sharing of memories, a leader, such as a pastor or the oldest child, will invite people to share memories. These moments at the graveside will be engraved on each person's heart.

I remember one occasion when the remaining spouse and the other siblings were elderly and therefore the funeral director had provided chairs for these people. The weather was perfect, and the funeral service had already happened. The funeral director and I waited at least thirty minutes as the immediate family shared memories. We couldn't leave because the family members needed the chairs. I give this example because it shows that we ought to share memories at important times—and one of those times is when we are gathered at the gravesite of our loved ones.

j. Visiting Nearby Graves

When family members and friends have been buried in the same cemetery as the person who is being buried now, it is natural that individuals will find the grave markers of these other people. As family members then reflect at these other graves, they will sense a spirit of community.

k. Sprinkling Sand on the Casket

I don't usually sprinkle sand on the coffin at a burial service. Here, though, I want to be sensitive to the family. On several occasions as I have said the words, "Ashes to ashes (when it is a cremation), dust to dust, earth to earth," I have carefully and slowly poured sand in the form of a cross and then a heart. The family saw the heart and the cross. They knew what these meant. Possibly those two images were remembered for a longer period of time than all of my words. A heart represents the love of the person in the coffin, and the cross represents the love of God, who is present with his comfort.

Reflections
• Which of these practices would you want for yourself?
• If you were planning the parts of your own burial service, what would you want your family to do to remember you?

Prayer
Heavenly Father, gathering at a graveside is the most solemn moment I might ever experience. I will feel my mortality and finiteness. The cemetery is a clear reminder that I will not be here forever. But, as a person who believes in you, I am confident that the cemetery is not an end. It is not a final stop. Yes, it is a final resting spot for my body—but just for a time. I have the assurance that it is only a resting place, knowing that when your trumpet will sound, I will be raised to new life, and I will be with you forever. May I therefore hold on to the assurance that a cemetery is just a stop in the journey towards my eternal home, where I will be with

you forever. May this assurance be evident in my burial service. In Jesus' name, Amen.

Chapter Six
Recognizing Family Brokenness

This chapter emphasizes the need to recognize personal brokenness that results in broken relationships. I will focus on providing hope in Chapters Eight, Nine, and Ten.

When a family gathers to plan a funeral service, this special event is an opportunity for caring, remembering, and even reconciliation if necessary. There might well be hurt and unresolved issues in many families. If so, a funeral will be an occasion that will expose the family brokenness and pain. Some might wish that other family members were more pleasant and considerate. The others might wish that the first group were more sensitive and understanding. The desired outcome is that there would be reconciliation, but often that does not happen. Yet, the family need to move ahead with planning a funeral service in a limited time, hopefully with an open hand and with faces towards one another. But, regrettably, funerals are often events when our hearts are closed, we don't listen to one another, and our faces are not towards each other.

Also, the person for whose funeral the family are gathering might have caused pain. A father might not have represented God as a loving, caring Father even though he claimed to believe in God. Wishing this had not happened will not make it disappear. Hurtful memories are not magically erased at the time of a funeral service. Unkind, judgmental words always hurt. Harsh criticisms and putdowns always destroy. A daughter might have conflicted feelings as she stands by the coffin containing the body of a father who controlled and abused her emotionally, physically, and sexually and demeaned his wife, her mother, who is standing beside her. She will not only have feelings of bitterness and regret towards her father but might also have feelings of disappointment towards her mother for not protecting her from a controlling and abusive father.

The truth of the proverb, "The tongue has the power of life or death" (Proverbs 18:21), is very evident as family members recall the impact of the words of their loved one. The father's words might have destroyed the happiness and the unity of a family. Often, specific children within the family felt the deadly impact of the father's words more than other children. Yet, these family members are called to grieve over the loss of the person who inflicted pain, abuse, and even emotional death.

As a pastor, there have been times when I was aware that parents had caused pain. In one story, the rift was so deep that some of the children were forbidden to attend the funeral of the first parent. Years later, the second parent died. This same family, with all its divisions, requested that I help them process the funeral for the second parent. What should I have said to these children as they planned the funeral service for their parent? Some people will answer that in a case like this I should not bring up any difficult issues. However, my silence might also speak volumes, especially when the family knows that I, as a pastor, am aware of the hurt within the family.

Families might or might not know that the pastor is aware of their family problems. In the above situation, I was aware of the deep hurt, and the family knew that I was familiar with the family's pain and divisions. I do not believe that I, as the pastor, should open a hurtful wound. But, if the family opens the subject, I need to listen and acknowledge their hurt. I cannot undo what has happened, but I can at least listen and acknowledge their pain.

The last thing children in such a situation need to hear are admonitions that they must forgive and forget, especially if I as a pastor use Bible verses to bring home the truth. They will have heard these verses already, possibly and regrettably from the person who abused them. Instead, the family members need to be assured that I, as a pastor, accept them where they are, with all of their hurts and raw emotions. If the family members are assured of this, then they will be in a better position to accept and receive the other things I will say, both in planning the service and then at the burial service and at the funeral itself.

> **Listening and Caring**
>
> A carpenter uses a hammer to pound in a nail. But may Bible verses never be pounded into the hearts of hurting people. The pain and grief will only go deeper. May we instead listen and sit with people in their hurt and pain.

I have included this chapter on "Recognizing Family Brokenness" because it is a necessary reminder to me and to every family. Satan will stop at nothing; his goal is to kill and destroy. Satan does not care whether a family is in intense grief. He does not care how great the loss is. Satan's goal is to destroy families at the most vulnerable and weakest moment in their lives. Satan will do all he can to drive a wedge between family members and to widen the gulf that separates family members.

If you are in a family that is struggling with divisions and hurt at the time of grief and loss, may you feel compassion and grace from your friends and from the church. Be assured that God is gracious, no matter how insensitive people are. My prayer is that Christians will demonstrate God's compassion as well as humility and the courage to admit wrong.

At the same time, a funeral service and the other events surrounding it can be an opportunity for significant victories and personal repentance and growth. Satan knows this as well. I have observed children and grandchildren recommitting their lives to God. I have witnessed family members who have not talked for years speaking to one another on the occasion of the funeral service of a parent. These can be occasions for reconciliation and healing of fractured relationships. I was humbled as a son challenged his siblings and nieces and nephews that it was now time for them to take up the baton of faith handed to them by their parents. Satan knows that funerals can be opportunities for believers to recommit themselves to God and for wayward children and grandchildren to come home to the faith of their parents. Satan will do all he can, by any means, to thwart the gracious, merciful, and convicting moving of God's Spirit. Therefore, we must be on our knees, both as those who are grieving and also as those who lead in these services.

Reflections

As you read this chapter on the topic of family brokenness, are you thinking ahead to the funeral of a loved one, a parent, or a sibling? Do you already feel the deep emotions that may surface? My wish is that you will be assured that God will be in that valley, God will be present in that very difficult time as you feel both deep grief and unresolved negative feelings. The truth of this saying applies at all times, but especially in times of grief and loss: "Hurting people deeply hurt hurting people." May you be spared any extra hurt.

Can you visualize the contrast between a clenched fist, ready to strike, and an open hand, ready to embrace? A funeral might not be the time to resolve all misunderstandings and bitterness, but may it be a time for you to offer an open hand, ready to embrace and accept and begin the journey of reconciliation. May you feel other people offering the same towards you.

Prayer

Heavenly Father, even as I reach up to you for forgiveness and acceptance in my grief, I observe the conflict and callousness towards my brothers and sisters who are with me in our common grief. In myself, I cannot bring about reconciliation. This is a miracle that only you can perform. I open myself up to you and desire that reconciliation will begin with me. May I and my brothers and sisters come to you, Jesus, and hear your tender voice inviting me, "Come to me, you who are burdened and heavy laden, and I will give you rest." I come with my guilt and shame. I ask for forgiveness and pray for humility to reach out to those I hurt. In Jesus' name, Amen.

Chapter Seven
Writing Our Life Story: A Personal and a Faith Legacy

Planning our funeral provides us with a unique opportunity to reflect on our own life journey. As we do so, we select the details we want included. This brings up the question: "What do we want to be remembered by?" The following section applies to individuals writing their own life stories and also to children who will write the life stories of their parents.

It is one thing to emphasize the importance of developing a complete, honest, and inspiring life story and to offer guidelines for doing so. It is an altogether different matter to develop such a story for oneself. That is to say, it is easier to give principles and guidelines than to follow them. However, I have made it my goal to write my own life story, and I challenge you, who are reading this chapter, to take the time to write your own life story.

I will first give underlying principles and values that can help to determine how to approach writing a life story. This is followed by some specific guidelines that will help in writing our life stories.

1. Principles and Values that Should Determine Our Approach

We no doubt know the line, "I'm only a sinner, saved by grace." This is certainly true for each of us. But is this really how we want to be remembered?

The Psalmist David openly admitted, "For I know my transgressions, and my sin is always before me. Against you, you only have I sinned and done what is evil in your sight" (Psalm 51:3-4). The Apostle Paul confessed, "I was once a blasphemer and a persecutor and a violent man....Christ Jesus came into the world to save sinners—of whom I am the worst. But for that very reason I was shown mercy, so that in me, the worst of sinners, Christ Jesus might display his unlimited patience as an example for those who would believe on him and receive eternal life" (1 Timothy 1:13, 15-16). David and Paul openly confessed who they had been and what they had done. However, David knew that because he had confessed his sin and then received cleansing and restoration from the Lord, he was able to say, "I will teach transgressors your ways, and sinners will turn back to you" (Psalm 51:13). Paul also knew that the transformation in his life, from persecutor to preacher, would bring glory to God. This is why he concluded his brief testimony by confessing that he had been a blasphemer and persecutor but also asserting that he was now an example of God's unlimited patience with these words of praise: "Now to the King eternal, immortal, invisible, the only God, be honor and glory for ever and ever. Amen" (1 Timothy 1:17).

I mention David's and Paul's testimonies because they challenge us to examine how and for what purpose we write our life stories and how children write about their parents. As I have read the accounts of people and the stories children write about their parents, I have become troubled. I ask myself and all of us who write these accounts:

• Why does it seem that we are intent on to making ourselves appear as sinners but also as heroes and saints?

• Why do we, as children, need to make our parents appear more perfect than they were?

• Why do we avoid talking about our brokenness, our pain, our failures, and our disabilities—even and especially when these happened after we began following Jesus?

Very seldom will a family member share how a parent acknowledged a weakness or even a sin and then asked for forgiveness. I believe I have yet to see a parent write that he needed to confess to his family and then seek forgiveness from his family. If the parent did this, it would reveal that God had brought healing within the family.

Yes, we need to honor our parents. However, we should also admit that they were not perfect. Often a family will share openly in my office. They will speak of the pain and heartache felt within the family. Yet, they will be very guarded as they write their parent's life story and then share it in the service. I am not suggesting that a funeral be the occasion to bring up unresolved and painful memories. I am thankful that I have heard such hurtful words being said on only a very few occasions. But I am encouraging us to consider the example of the Psalmist who cried to God in his struggles, the example of Jeremiah who shared his questions, even his lamentations, and the example of the Apostle Paul who prayed that God would remove his "thorn in the flesh." We note:

• Lament Psalms are the most frequent of all types of Psalms.

• Jeremiah described his struggles and questions in Jeremiah 36-38 and elsewhere.

• Paul candidly acknowledged struggles with his vision and the thorn in his side (2 Corinthians 11:16-12:10).

With each of these men, we need to recognize our weakness and frailty but also God's compassion and strength.

Our reluctance to be honest makes me wonder:

• Would our life story not bring more glory to God if we shared our struggles and doubts and not only our accomplishments and victories?

• Would our children not honor their parents even more than they do now if we shared how we, their parents, were prone to fail and how we struggled yet kept on striving in our brokenness, rather than describing only our victories and achievements?

• Would such a life story not be more honest and also give us all hope—as we envision God softening our hearts as well as the hearts of the people we are concerned about?

• Would a life story that includes examples of brokenness and vulnerability not bring hope to those who follow us, in that it will show we are all broken and vulnerable, we all fail, and we all need restoration and healing?

• Would we, as those who follow Jesus, not rather strive to be those who stoop down and take a basin and wash each other's feet? (John 13) I note this for two reasons: first, many of our parents humbly followed Jesus by caring and doing the menial task; and second, this is a reason we need to honor them.

Many, if not most, of the people at a funeral service likely already know painful truths about the loved one. Questions I ask are:

• Do we need to present only the pleasant and positive experiences in our lives and in our families?

• Have we portrayed a Christianity where God cannot deal with our pain and brokenness?

• Do we honestly believe our God is the strong and faithful Good Shepherd who will never leave us, even as we stumble and fall? Do we really believe he stays with us as we live as broken people in broken families, in valleys of despair and discouragement, in valleys of death and hopelessness?

May God give us grace and humility to recognize our failures and our frailty.

The Psalmist David and the Apostle Paul shared how God transformed their lives, how God was there when they failed, and then how God turned them around, from rejecting God to repentance and recommitment to God. The prophet Malachi prophesied that a core marker of revival is that the Lord "will turn the hearts of the fathers to their children, and the hearts of the children to their fathers" (Malachi 4:6). I wish that our lives, and then our life stories, would contain many examples of such revivals in our families. May we have the humility to document how God restores and heals broken fathers, mothers, and whole families.

This brings to mind Jesus' calling of Matthew, a despised tax collector—a man the religious leaders dismissed as "a sinner." Jesus' response applies to all of us, as he said, "I desire mercy, not sacrifice. For I have not come to call the righteous, but sinners" (Matthew 9:13).

I urge all of us to become more honest and humble as we write our life stories. None of us, certainly not we who are parents, are perfect. We are not heroes, even if we are tempted to present ourselves as such. We all struggle in life.

I invite us to hear the words of W. H. Auden: "To a Christian the godlike man is not the hero who does extraordinary things, but the holy man who does good deeds" (James M. Houston, *Joyful Exiles*, 34). My appeal is that we not present ourselves as heroes. My wish is that our children will not feel pressured to present us as heroes but to celebrate the times we expressed our love of Jesus with our good deeds.

I further invite us to hear the words of creation, when God, our Creator, declared that we, his creation, are "very good." The Bible affirms the essential worth and significance of each person because we all are created in God's image. Our value does not diminish when we stumble and fall. We have incomparable worth in God's eyes, as we are created in his image and called by him to fulfill what he desires (Genesis 1:26-31, Psalm 139). My appeal is that we never diminish our value, or the value of our loved ones, but affirm their worth because it is given by God. Our worth is a given; it is no less when we fail, and no more when we have achieved great accomplishments. May none of us ever say, "I have nothing to write about my life because I accomplished nothing extraordinary."

I invite us to hear the words of Paul that we are partners with God (Philippians 1:4-6) and ambassadors for God (2 Corinthians 5:20) in the work God is doing. This applies also to our parents who were committed to be faithful, obedient servants. Most of our parents were certainly not distinguished as exceptional heroes. It is enough that they were faithful with what God had entrusted to them. My appeal is that we affirm them as faithful co-workers and partners with God. This is of far greater significance than any worldly achievement they may or may not have accomplished.

I invite us to hear the words of Micah: "He has showed you, O man, what is good. And what does the LORD require of you? To act justly and to love mercy and to walk humbly with your God" (Micah 6:8). My appeal is that we celebrate how our parents did what the Lord required and how they walked humbly before God.

I invite us to hear the words of Jesus: "Blessed are the poor in spirit...those who mourn...the meek...those who hunger and thirst for righteousness...[and] those who are persecuted because of righteousness" (Matthew 5:3-12). My appeal is that we celebrate how our parents demonstrated these godly qualities.

Even more, my appeal is that we seek to write our life stories and our parents' life stories as expressions of our faith journeys where the focus will be to honor God. When we share how God is transforming us, then God will receive the glory.

This brings in another matter. Unless we have such an approach to our life stories and our parents' life stories, unless we see our lives through the above lens, then we will have the following dilemma. We will divide humanity into sinners and saints, failures and heroes, the unknown and the celebrities—and bypass the first group and exalt the second.

> **A Suicide's Life Story**
> My invitation is that we consider how we write our life story and the stories of our loved ones. We want to do so with a sense of God's grace and compassion. May we maintain this stance even with individuals who have committed suicide. This might be seen as an extreme example, but, unless we can embrace every person with God's grace, then we will not embrace any person with God's grace—beginning with ourselves. The love of God extends to every person, even those who felt their lives were useless and took their own lives.

2. Guidelines for Writing Life Stories

We might agree that we need to write our life story while we are still able to. Or our children might recognize that they want to write a life story for their mother or father at the parent's funeral. But the question then is: "How do we go about writing a life story? What should be included?" This will be either our question or our children's question. There are resources available that help us record our life events and story. For the sake of writing a life story that will be intended for a funeral, I suggest that we see our lives in several arenas as well as several cycles.

a. Life Arenas: Family, Career, Faith, Leisure

A life story will normally begin with the person's family of origin. Then we will want to note key experiences within the family—as children, youth, adults, and retirees. We will also wish to reflect on the other three arenas: career, faith, leisure.

b. Life Cycles: Transitions and Stages

Stages are those phases in life that are linked together by transitions. Another way to understand transitions is that they are like bridges connecting stages. Some key transitions are adolescence, moving out of the home of origin, marriage, having children, mid-life decision-making, children leaving home, pre-retirement, and retirement. The ideal is to perceive these transitions as a challenge, an opportunity for growth. Richard P. Johnson explains how to write an autobiography, either an older person writing his or her own story or children helping their elderly parents write their stories. The children's goal is to help their aging parents have a more positive and meaningful attitude (Richard P. Johnson, *How to Honor Your Aging Parents*, 1999]).

As we begin writing our own autobiography or as our children begin writing our life story, it will be obvious that life has not always been as we had hoped. We will not be able to change our life history, but we can choose how we will write our life story. The ideal is that we will regularly reflect on our lives. When we write our life story, we will consciously review our lives. The concern then is: how will we review or reflect on our lives, especially when our lives contain pain and tragedy and not only pleasant and enjoyable moments? An answer is given by the Apostle Paul in his letter to the believers in Thessalonica: "Be joyful always; pray continually; give thanks in all circumstances, for this is God's will for you in Christ Jesus" (1 Thessalonians 5:16-18). If we are to have a Christian perception of our lives, we will follow these three directives given by the Apostle Paul. Paul is clear that this "is God's will for us in Christ Jesus." I will comment on each directive as it applies to our life stories.

First, we should "be joyful always." Joy is the product of seeing that God was and is in our lives. Joy is the result of knowing God's presence now and knowing that he was near in the past (Psalm 16:11, Acts 2:25).

Second, we should "give thanks in all circumstances." Gratitude is the God-lens through which we should see our lives. How we see our lives will shape our lives. We need to understand that our life is a gift, not a reward. This is especially pertinent when we look back over our lives. We are

> As we look back in life, may we:
> • be joyful always;
> • pray continually;
> • give thanks in all circumstances.
> (1 Thessalonians 5:16-18)

not the source of the things we have done or accomplished. We have been and will always be dependent on our God. Gratitude is the way to see our lives as something God has bestowed.

When we follow these two instructions by the Apostle Paul, we will become aware that we have reasons to be joyful and grateful as we write our life story. This is possible when we see God's presence in our lives. However, these two qualities do not come naturally nor easily. How can we have this perspective to see our lives as God's gift to us?

Third, I believe the answer is given by the Apostle Paul in his third directive: "pray continually." When we pray, we give ourselves the time to be in God's presence, to hear his loving voice, to feel his tender touch. As we pray, we will recognize we have much to be grateful for and many reasons to be joyful. The more we pray, the more joyful and grateful we will be.

When we take the time to be in God's presence through prayer, we will see our lives, no matter what they included, as times when God was present and therefore as full of reasons to thank God. Then, writing our life story will not be perceived as a negative chore or a duty that is required for the sake of a funeral program. We will be motivated by gratitude to God, and our stories will be filled with the sweet aroma of joy and thanksgiving.

In summary, my desire is that my life journey, when it is written, either by myself or by my children, will only glorify God and not draw attention to myself. When people look at me, or at any of us, may they see my brokenness, my stumbling, and my flaws. But may they then know that I knelt at the cross. Then, may they see me through Jesus' lens. May they see that I was continually in God's presence through prayer. May they see a joyful and a grateful spirit.

With the Apostle Paul, may this commitment be true for each of us: "For to me, to live is Christ, and to die is gain" (Philippians 1:21).

Reflections

• How do I honestly wish to be remembered—as an outstanding hero or as a humble, faithful follower of Jesus?

• What might it look like for me to come to a place where I accept my worth?

• This also applies to my loved ones: Possibly, in many people's perception, my parents are seen as failures, as people who neither succeeded nor achieved anything significant. How can I recognize their worth and have the courage to declare this publicly?

• As I reflect on my life story, are there things that I sense I would still like to do?

• The concept of a "bucket list" might come to mind—things I wish to do or places I wish to see. Often a "bucket list" is perceived as containing things people want to do for themselves. As we review our lives, my wish is that we see this list as things we want to do for other people, relationships we wish to restore, or attitudes we need to pursue. Make a (bucket) list of things such as:

  • relationships I need to restore
  • my life story that needs to be written
  • a volunteer ministry I will commit to

Prayer

Heavenly Father, as I have read this chapter on writing a life story, this has invited me to look in the mirror. I ask myself: how do I want to be remembered? I realize that I cannot undo how I have lived. But, as of this day, may my deepest desire be to simply follow Jesus closely—to hear his voice and see his eye on me. As I look back, may I have the clarity to see your faithfulness, your compassion, and your constant care. May I then write my life story so that my children and other people will also receive hope for their lives. May they see how you have been faithful to your covenant with me and that you will be faithful to your covenant with them. Then, as I look ahead in the remaining days you have for me, may I have the courage to obey, even when you lead into new paths of obedience. May I constantly renew my commitment to follow Jesus with all my heart, my mind, and my soul. In Jesus' name, Amen.

Chapter Eight
Assurance that We Will Cross the Finish Line to Eternal Life

The title of this book is taken from the Apostle Paul's reflection on his life. He looked back and with assurance declared, "I have fought the good fight, I have finished the race, I have kept the faith" (2 Timothy 4:6). I am drawing on Paul's phrase, "finished the race," for the image of "crossing the finish line."

We watch with anticipation as runners in the summer Olympic games approach the finish line. The metaphor of the twenty-six mile-marathon race fits this book. In the long marathon race, we cheer as runners endure, right to the finish line. At a funeral service, we celebrate how a loved one endured and, in the Apostle Paul's words, "finished the race and kept the faith." We also rejoice because the Lord, the righteous Judge, has "in store the crown of righteousness" for "all who have longed for his appearing" (2 Timothy 4:6-8).

It is one thing to focus on funeral services, burial services, and the important decisions that need to be made at the time of a person's death. However, it is much more important that each of us, including the person whose funeral we are celebrating, will cross the finish line from life on earth to life in heaven. By "crossing the finish line," we do not simply mean that we will take our last breath and then complete our life here on earth.

We will cross the finish line when we:
- believe in Jesus
- follow Jesus
- desire to be with Jesus
- are the bride of Jesus.

However, as with any metaphor, comparing our lives to a marathon also has shortcomings or limitations. I will answer the question, "How can I be assured I will cross the finish line?" using several additional biblical metaphors. This approach is necessary because it is biblical. The Apostle Paul, who used the marathon metaphor, also used other ways to describe the Christian life. The Bible describes the people who follow Jesus in various ways—as those who believe in Jesus, as those who follow Jesus, as those who look to the prize he has for them, as Jesus' bride, as those who are committed to do his will. As I briefly explain each, it will become clear that these are interrelated. This means that a person who believes in Jesus will follow him, love him, and serve him.

1. A Believer in Jesus is Assured to Cross the Finish Line.

We begin with the question: "Can we take for granted that everyone will cross from this life to the next in heaven?" This question can also be restated as, "Will everyone be in heaven once they die?"

Jesus spoke to the concern that not everyone will automatically cross from this life to an eternal life with God in heaven. He did so in his conversation with Nicodemus. Jesus said, "Whoever believes in him (Jesus himself) is not condemned, but whoever does not believe stands condemned already because he has not believed in the name of God's one and only Son" (John 3:18). The answer to the question, "Will everyone cross the finish line and be in heaven once they die?" is a serious and solemn "No!" Based on Jesus' words, those who believe in him will cross the finish line into heaven and be in God's eternal presence, but those who do not believe in him will not cross the finish line into heaven.

Jesus provided a solution so that everyone is able to cross the finish line. The angel Gabriel instructed Joseph to name his son Jesus because "he will save his people from their sins" (Matthew 1:21). When Jesus died on the cross, he died as the Lamb of God who took away the sin of the world (John 1:29). So, Jesus provided a solution to enable everyone to cross the finish line, but not everyone will do so. This takes us to another question: "How can *we* be assured we will cross the heavenly finish line?"

Jesus' words give us the answer: "For God so loved the world that he gave his one and only Son, that whoever believes in him shall not perish but have eternal life. For God did not send his Son into the world to condemn the world, but to save the world through him" (John 3:16-17). The essential requirement is belief in Jesus. The Apostle John emphasized the importance of belief in Jesus: "And this is the testimony: God has given us eternal life, and this life is in his Son. He who has the Son has life; he who does not have the Son of God does not have life" (1 John 5:11-12).

John also clearly stated that we can be confident we will cross the finish line: "I write these things to you who believe in the name of the Son of God so that you may know that you have eternal life" (1 John 5:13).

2. A Follower of Jesus Is Assured to Cross the Finish Line.

We have noted that the core requirement to be in heaven is belief in Jesus. But the Bible teaches that belief in Jesus is not merely an acknowledgment of various facts about Jesus. Sometimes this is described as mere "believism." A person who truly believes in Jesus will follow him in life. This becomes clear in these points:

a. Belief in Jesus Is Not Merely Familiarity with or Perception of a Fact.

James wrote, "What good is it, my brothers, if a man claims to have faith but has no deeds? Can such faith save him?...In the same way, faith by itself, if it is not accompanied by action, is dead....You believe that there is one God. Good! Even the demons believe that—and shudder" (James 2:14, 17, 19).

b. Belief in Jesus Will Be Evident in Obedience.

Jesus himself said, "Not everyone who says to me, 'Lord, Lord,' will enter the kingdom of heaven, but only he who does the will of my Father who is in heaven. Many will say to me on that day, 'Lord, Lord, did we not prophesy in your name, and in your name drive out demons and perform many miracles?' Then I will tell them plainly, 'I never knew you. Away from me, you evildoers!'" (Matthew 7:21-23).

c. Belief in Jesus Will Be Demonstrated in How We Treat Others.

Our belief in Jesus will be evident in that we will treat people as if they were Jesus. Our relationship to Jesus will be evident in how we treat the marginalized and vulnerable, the frail and the defenseless. Jesus said that when he returned in glory, he would divide people based on how they treated those who were hungry, thirsty, without clothes, sick, and in prison. (Matthew 25:31-46). James taught: "Religion that God our Father accepts as pure and faultless is this: to look after orphans and widows in their distress" (James 1:27).

d. Belief in Jesus Will Be Evident in Our Relationships.

The Apostle John wrote: "And this is his command: to believe in the name of his Son, Jesus Christ, and to love one another as he commanded us" (1 John 3:23).

e. Belief in Jesus Will Be Evident in Our Longing for His Appearance.

Those who truly believe in Jesus will display a constant expectation, anticipation, and longing for his appearance. Jesus told us: "Therefore keep watch, because you do not know the day or the hour" (Matthew 25:1-13). He also said, "Do not let your heart be troubled. Trust in God, trust also in me. In my Father's house are many rooms; if it were not so, I would have told you. I am going there to prepare a place for you. And if I go and prepare a place for you, I will come back and take you to be with me that you may be there I am. You know the way to the place where I am going" (John 14:1-4).

f. Belief in Jesus Will Be Evident in Our Waiting for the Fulfilment of His Promises.

Those who have faith in Jesus say with confidence: "I will dwell in the house of the LORD forever" (Psalm 23:6). This hinges on the relationship we have with our Lord, that he is "our Shepherd" (Psalm 23:1).

g. Belief in Jesus Will Be Evident in that We Are Following Him.

When we are followers of Jesus, it means that we have heard and accepted his invitation: "Come, follow me, and I will make you fishers of men" (Mark 1:17). This means that Jesus is the Rabbi and we are his disciples, his followers. He calls us to be with him, to follow him, to feel his heart, to know his mind, to understand and do his will, and to follow his directions in all areas of our lives.

Therefore, crossing the finish line from here to eternity means that, as we have sought to follow him here on this earth and as we have prayed that his will be done in our lives now, he is inviting us to an even greater union with him forever, where nothing will hinder our complete desire to follow him in all eternity.

3. Those Who Look Forward to the Prize Jesus Has for Them Are Assured to Cross the Finish Line.

While keeping the metaphor of a marathon, I believe we need to add another perspective to it. In a marathon, the normal concern is to run from a starting point, remain on the prescribed track, and reach the finish line. The emphasis is on the race, and usually very little mention is made of the prize for having reached the finish line. Yet, when this metaphor is applied to our lives, the focus is not merely on following some prescribed rules from birth until death, and then it is all over. In many marathons, the runners will receive some item to recognize that they have successfully completed the race. But here is where we need to add the extra element when applying the marathon metaphor to our lives. We not only run the race according to the rules Jesus gives. There is also a prize waiting for us at the other side of the finish line.

The author of the book of Hebrews wrote about this prize when he wrote that "man is destined to die once, and after that to face judgment" (Hebrews 9:27). This judgment is God's final verdict on each person. The rest of the sentence gives clarity to the issue of whether everyone who dies will be in heaven. The sentence continues: "so Christ was sacrificed once to take away the sins of many people; and he will appear a second time, not to bear sin, but to bring salvation to those who are waiting for him." The text states that Christ will bring salvation only to those "who are waiting for him." This points to the critical issue of whether a person is waiting for Jesus. This means we can say that we will cross from life on earth to life in heaven if we are waiting for Jesus. He is the ultimate prize we are longing for.

The Bible has numerous places where the prize on the other side of the finish line, the other side of death, is mentioned. These are only a sample of verses describing the major incentive and enticement God is giving us as we follow him:
• a crown that lasts forever (1 Corinthians 9:25).
• the crown of righteousness that the Lord will award (2 Timothy 4:8).
• the crown of life that God has promised to those who love him (James 1:12).
• the crown of glory that will never fade away (1 Peter 5:4).
• the right to eat from the tree of life (Revelation 2:7).
• a white stone with a new name written on it, known only to him who receives it (Revelation 2:17).

In summary, we are assured that we will cross the finish line when our goal is not the finish line but is beyond the finish line. Our goal is to be with Jesus, in the home he is now preparing for us (John 14:1-3).

Our longing to cross the finish line and be with Jesus is taken to a much higher level in the next basis of assurance.

4. A Lover of Jesus (His Bride) Will be Assured to Cross the Finish Line.

I want to conclude with another metaphor that applies to the end of life. The primary one in this book is that we are runners, striving to cross the finish line of a marathon and then receive the prize on the other side. But there are other metaphors in the Bible that are more prominent and certainly more inspiring than a marathon.

This next metaphor adds an altogether more appealing description of what it means to cross the finish line. It takes crossing the finish line to a new and exciting level. The moment of crossing the finish line is much more than a final gasp, expending the last vestige of our strength in a strenuous effort to make it. The Bible describes this moment with a much nobler image. It pictures the finish line as the beginning of a wedding celebration. This changes how we perceive ourselves here and for all eternity. Our lives are a marathon, but much more. They are meant to be a wedding preparation. Let me explain.

On Jesus' last evening with his disciples, the Thursday evening before his crucifixion, he used the following image. He pictured himself as a groom, engaged to a bride, his people. He assured the disciples, and therefore all who follow Jesus, that at this time he is building the home he wants us to live in with him. Picture this familiar passage with this understanding: "Do not let your hearts be troubled. Trust in God; trust also in me. In my Father's house are many rooms; if it were not so, I would have told you. I am going there to prepare a place for you. And if I go and prepare a place for you, I will come back and take you to be with me that you also may be where I am. You know the way to the place where I am going....I am the way and the truth and the life. No one comes to the Father except through me" (John 14:1-4, 6). This means that Jesus, as the groom, is now building a room in his Father's house for his bride. We can be assured of crossing the finish line and being with Jesus in heaven if we are his bride.

This brings us to the most critical question: "How do I know I am Jesus' bride?" The answer includes all that has been said thus far. I am assured that I am the bride of Christ if:

• I believe what the Bible says, that Jesus is the Son of God, that he is the only Savior of the world, that he came to give his life to pay for my sins, and that he rose from the dead to give me eternal life.

• I confess that I have rejected God, that I am a sinner, and that Jesus died for me.

• I believe that Jesus rose from the dead and, because of that belief, I am assured that he is now living in me. This gives me eternal life.

• I have accepted Jesus' invitation, "Come, follow me, and I will make you fishers of men." Since I have accepted Jesus' invitation to follow him, this means that I will take up my cross, I will desire to know him intimately, I will accept his teachings, and I will do what he commands.

• I believe Jesus is now preparing a room in his Father's house for me. Therefore, I am living in anticipation of the day Jesus will call me to be with him.

In the answer I have outlined to the question, "How do I know I am Jesus' bride?" I need to add this clarification to what is meant by the words "I believe." We usually think of the word "believe" as an affirmation of some mental thought. We think "head knowledge." Then, we may infer that all we need to do is accept or believe in the proofs or teachings in the Bible or the statements someone points out to us and we will be saved. Or, staying with the metaphor of the bride and the bridegroom, we conclude that we are the bride of Jesus simply because we believe specific Bible teachings. However, in the language of the Bible, and in the way Jesus and the disciples and apostles used the notion of believing, this had to do with matters of the heart and the will—trusting and surrendering oneself fully to another person. Keeping the metaphor of marriage, as a husband, I do not merely accept some truths in my head about my wife. Our relationship is much deeper. It involves our will, our emotions, our desire to be committed to one another, our commitment to love one another, and our promise to express this passionately. This certainly applies to our understanding of what it means that we are the bride and Jesus is the bridegroom.

Here I want to return to the theme of this chapter, this is, being assured that a person will cross the finish line. If you have any doubt whether you are Jesus' bride, and therefore you are unsure if you are prepared to cross the finish line when you die, the following is a second part of the answer to the question, "How do I know I am Jesus' bride?"

The answer is that you will want to do what a bride does—that is, get herself ready for her wedding. The last pages of the Bible speak about a wedding celebration that will last for all eternity. A word that is repeated is, "Come!" God's people, Jesus' bride, long for him to come. The last words that Jesus' followers say in the Bible is, "Amen. Come, Lord Jesus" (Revelation 22:17, 20). You will know, without any doubt, that you are prepared to cross the finish line when your deepest longing is, "Come, Lord Jesus!" You will know that you are prepared to die and be with Jesus when you long to be with Jesus and are living with his coming in view.

This gives us a new perception of what it means to be prepared to cross the finish line. When we cross the finish line, we enter the wedding hall to participate in the greatest wedding celebration ever.

In summary, how can I be assured I will cross the finish line to be with Jesus? As noted briefly above, the Bible provides many teachings that answer this question: To be able to cross the finish line, I will believe Jesus for who he says he is. Therefore, I will follow him in all areas of life. Further, I will look beyond the finish line to the promise that I will be with Jesus forever. And I will love him because he has chosen me to be part of his bride and I want to enjoy the wedding celebration with him.

Reflections

The most important thing in this life is that you are prepared to be with Jesus in heaven. The Bible provides many verses that explain what it means to become a follower of Jesus. My chief concern is that you have clarity on this matter, based on what the Bible states. The core issue is that you can say with confidence, "I believe in Jesus, the Son of God, and therefore I know I have eternal life." But I need to underscore that believing in Jesus is much more than head knowledge and checking a box mentally that says something such as, "Jesus is God, Jesus died for my sins, and some day I'll be with Jesus." Believing in Jesus involves trusting and surrendering our all, giving our allegiance to the kingdom of God and living out that commitment in our lives.

If there is any doubt as to whether you are prepared to die and be with Jesus, I am offering a prayer you could make your own. These words are an opportunity to express what is in your heart. Read this prayer over. If it captures where your heart and mind are right now, then make these words your prayer. May this be your prayer to God.

Prayer

Dear God: Thank you for your love for me. I have been thinking about funeral plans. But the most important thing is that I am prepared to meet you and be with you forever. Therefore, I know I must follow what is written in your Word, the Bible. The Bible says that I am a sinner—I have rejected you. I confess that I have lived in rebellion, as a sinner. The Bible also says that Jesus came for sinners like me, that he died to pay the penalty for my sins. I believe in Jesus, that what he did on the cross was for me. The Bible says that Jesus rose to new life. I believe that Jesus is now living in me. Even more, I believe Jesus is preparing a home for me in heaven. As I long for his return, I am committed to follow Jesus in everything I do and say. God, there is much more I could say, but thank you for making me your child. Even more, thank you for making me a part of the bride of Jesus. This is more than I can imagine. Thank you. Thank you, Jesus.

Chapter Nine

Restoring Hope and Acceptance of the Present as We Near the Finish Line

Being prepared to cross the finish line from this life to eternal life with Jesus for all eternity includes much more than making all the important funeral arrangements. Certainly, it is wise to plan all the many details as we look forward to the time God will call us home. The previous chapter focused on the need to be at peace with God. However, my understanding is that we will only have complete peace with God when we have peace with all the people in our relationships. Only then will we have the assurance that we will cross the finish line.

Therefore, there are three further aspects I wish to mention that are related to being prepared to cross the finish line. These three aspects are that we will restore hope and acceptance as we near the finish line, that we will restore peace in our relationships, and that we will run the race and cross the finish line in community. These are the topics of the next three chapters.

The central metaphor in this manual is that our lives are like a long marathon. In any marathon, the last section is often the most difficult, the portion of the race where the runners doubt whether they will make it to the finish line. In a marathon, the runners need to accept the challenges that come in the last few miles and even the last few feet. Similarly, we need to recognize the challenges that the final years and months in our lives present. It is of no value to refuse to recognize these challenges, to wish it was otherwise, or even to deny or ignore what is happening. In this chapter, I will note that there is an attitude that applies towards the end of life that is necessary to help us be prepared to cross the finish line. This attitude is an acceptance of the present—being at peace with the current reality of life because we believe it is lived under God.

In order to illustrate what is meant by accepting the present with all its challenges and trials, we turn to the Apostle Paul. Paul described a particular hardship he was in with these words: "We were under great pressure, far beyond our ability to endure, so that we despaired even of life" (2 Corinthians 1:8). Paul did not describe this life-threatening hardship. Later, he wrote about a time when he was "harassed at every turn—conflicts on the outside, fears within" (2 Corinthians 7:5). In our last stage of life, we might feel as the Apostle Paul felt. We could be afraid that we might not make it. Life is overwhelming, and all we seem to see are our challenges and our failures.

A personal incident in university illustrates the need to recognize what is actually happening towards the end of life. It clarifies that, with God's strength and the support of others, we can make the necessary changes and endure to the finish line. As I look back, I realize it was only a minor challenge, but it serves as an illustration that, when it seemed I was a failure and would not make it, there was still hope. I was writing my first essay in a third-year English class. When the professor returned my essay, two things jumped out. One was all the red marks on the paper (it seemed there was more red than black). The second thing was a note at the end: "Come to my office." I was extremely discouraged, but, with some hesitation, I went to see the professor. He kindly and thoroughly went through the paper, giving corrections and suggestions. His red marks were about grammar and style of writing and not the content itself. I reworked the paper, and this time there were only a few red marks. Then I wrote it a third time and received a satisfactory grade.

The comparison of the essay to the end of life is this. When we look back on our lives, certainly we will see all types of regrets, failures, missed opportunities, and broken promises. We might be filled with shame, regret, disappointment, and maybe even depression. Satan wants to paralyze us so that we see no hope, no possibility of going ahead, and no point in even attempting to go forward. We might believe we have only a few more years left, but we feel immobilized. We see only the mistakes we have made. Other people, friends as well as family members, remind us of all that we did wrong or should have done better. We hear sermons pointing to what we should aspire toward. We agree that we need to change—and we want to—yet our life appears like that essay. All we see are the red marks—failures, mistakes, shattered dreams, and broken promises. Life appears hopeless. We feel dark despair. However, just like that kind and wise professor, God both knows all our failures and desires to come alongside us and give us hope.

In this chapter I wish to point to three sources of hope. Just as a marathon runner will reach for a power drink as she comes towards the end of the marathon, take hold of these three truths.

1. Enjoy the Present—It is a Gift of God

The first source of hope might not be perceived as a source of hope. I am referring to the familiar words, "Eat, drink, and be merry." These words can be spoken with two very contrasting attitudes. We are perhaps more familiar with the first attitude than the second. The first attitude is given in the story Jesus told about a rich farmer. When this proud farmer looked over his bumper crop, he folded his hands, calculated that his barns would not store all his crops, and said to himself, "You have plenty of good things laid up for many years. Take life easy; eat, drink and be merry." God confronted this man with the words, "You fool! This very night your life will be demanded from you....This is how it will be with anyone who stores up things for himself but is not rich toward God" (Luke 12:16-21). That rich fool demonstrated greed, pride, and independence from God and from other people. The Bible is certainly not advocating this attitude.

However, the Bible encourages us to use the same words, "Eat, drink and be merry," but from a different source of strength and dependency. These same words are given by "the Teacher, son of David, king in Jerusalem" in the wisdom book of Ecclesiastes. Solomon, the acknowledged author, was able to acquire everything he desired— wisdom, pleasure, achievements, and riches. But he recognized that these were all meaningless and purposeless when they were achieved without God or without a sense of dependence on God. However, when life, with all it contains, is received as a gift from a loving God, it will bring joy. The following words contain the theme of the book of Ecclesiastes: "A man can do nothing better than to eat and drink and find satisfaction in his work. This too, I see, is from the hand of God, for without him, who can eat or find enjoyment? To the man who pleases him, God gives wisdom, knowledge and happiness, but to the sinner he gives the task of gathering and storing up wealth to hand it over to the one who pleases God" (Ecclesiastes 2:24-26). The book of Ecclesiastes contains the reflections of an old man. This is evident in the final chapter (12:1-7). Therefore, Solomon's deliberations are a necessary reminder to older people who need hope, especially when they come to the end of their lives. If you are elderly and have reached many goals and accomplished much, or if you are elderly and life has seemed to be one failure after another, hear these words again, as coming from another elderly person at the end of life: "Then I realized that it is good and proper for a man to eat and drink, and to find satisfaction in his toilsome labor under the sun during the few days of life God has given him—for this is his lot. Moreover, when God gives any man wealth and possessions, and enables him to enjoy them, to accept his lot and be happy in his work—this is a gift of God" (Ecclesiastes 5:18-19); "So I commend the enjoyment of life, because nothing is better for a man under the sun than to eat and drink and be glad. Then joy will accompany him in his work all the days of the life God has given him under the sun" (Ecclesiastes 8:15).

The first source of hope is given by an old man: "Eat, drink and be glad. Recognize that God is in control. Life is a gift from him, and he wishes the best for us." Life is a gift from God. This might be easier to accept when a person is young and healthy. But even when a person is elderly and is afflicted with pain and weakness, life is still a gift from God. Therefore, enjoy life, even with all the limitations. That is easier said than done, but take this advice from an older person like yourself—Solomon. And these are the words I, as a person in the last third of my life, want to say to myself.

2. Accept the Present with Gratitude

This second source of hope is actually another way to describe the first. When we accept life as a gift from God, then we will receive the here and now with gratitude. This might be very difficult as we become weaker and have more aches, pains, and diseases. Yet, when an attitude of gratitude has been cultivated earlier in life, this attitude will sustain us in the frailty of our final years.

I recall visiting an old gentleman. His body was filled with arthritis, he could hardly get up, and he needed assistance with the basic necessities of life. When I asked how he was, he said, "I've much to be thankful for. Better than I deserved."

I have been humbled and inspired by a similar attitude in other men and

> **The choice is ours:**
> • Gratitude or grumbling
> • Acceptance or resentment
> • Joy or complaining
> • Highlighting solutions or pointing at problems
> • Giving light or spreading gloom

women, facing increasing pain, limited by disability, feeling chronic discomfort, and being extremely frail. When I approach older people, I might expect to encounter a very different attitude and brace myself to hear a litany of complaints. But they often breathe gratitude. May their gratitude inspire each of us!

May we all face the present increasing frailty with dependence on God and then with gratitude. This requires deliberate and constant thankfulness. It's not easy, but you can have this attitude.

3. Trust in God's Constant Care, Right to the End

The third source of hope is related to the first two. Since our Lord is in control, and since we have so much to thank him for, we therefore will want to trust him—even when uncertainty seems to be overwhelming us like a threatening storm.

If any of you who are reading this book are nearing the end of life and feel discouraged, hear these words by the prophet Isaiah: "I said, 'I have labored to no purpose; I have spent my strength in vain and for nothing. Yet what is due me is in the LORD's hand, and my reward is with my God.' And now the LORD says...'Though [a mother] may forget, I will not forget you! See, I have engraved you on the palms of my hands; your walls are ever before me'" (Isaiah 49:4, 15-16). We might sense that all our life work has been in vain and for nothing and that our family and friends have forsaken us. May we then hear the assurance that what is due to us is in the Lord's hand and our reward is with our God, for he has engraved us on the palms of his hands.

> What's in our hearts will give us hope: "Above all else, guard your heart, for it is the wellspring of life" (Proverbs 4:23).

As we come to what we perceive as the final lap of life, we might be filled with an assortment of negative emotions—failure, anger, shame, guilt, blaming, disappointment. Yes, we will want to name and confess these. But then I invite us to see our God, to sense his compassionate eyes on us, to experience his open embrace. He wants to walk with us even— and especially—in our frailty and weakness. He has a good life for us to enjoy even now. We know it is good because God is good. See God as gracious, with open arms. Feel God's unconditional love and embrace.

Reflections

An expression that I have found insightful over the last years of life is this: "The way I lean is how I will fall." As I examine my attitudes over against the three sources of hope, how am I leaning?
• Am I enjoying the present, recognizing it is a gift of God?
• Am I accepting the present with gratitude?
• Am I trusting in God's constant care, right to the end?

When physical and emotional challenges weigh us down, it is necessary to fill our minds with promises. The following are some promises that will give hope and peace:
• "Even to your old age and gray hairs I am he, I am he who will sustain you. I have made you and I will carry you; I will sustain you and I will rescue you" (Isaiah 46:4).
• "But now, this is what the LORD says—he who created you, O Jacob, he who formed you, O Israel: 'Fear not, for I have redeemed you; I have

summoned you by name and you are mine. When you pass through the waters, I will be with you; and when you pass through the rivers, they will not sweep over you. When you walk through the fire, you will not be burned; the flames will not set you ablaze. For I am the LORD your God, the Holy One of Israel, your savior'" (Isaiah 43:1-2).

• "Why do you say, O Jacob, and complain, O Israel, 'My way is hidden from the LORD; my cause is disregarded by my God'? Do you not know? Have you not heard? The LORD is the everlasting God, the Creator of the ends of the earth. He will not grow tired or weary, and his understanding no one can fathom. He gives strength to the weary and increases the power of the weak. Even youths grow tired and weary, and young men stumble and fall; but those who hope in the LORD will renew their strength. They will soar on wings like eagles; they will run and not grow weary, they will walk and not be faint" (Isaiah 40:27-31).

• "'I said, "You are my servant"; I have chosen you and have not rejected you. So do not fear, for I am with you; do not be dismayed, for I am your God. I will strengthen you and help you; I will uphold you with my righteous right hand….For I am the LORD, your God, who takes hold of your right hand and says to you, Do not fear; I will help you. Do not be afraid, O worm Jacob, O little Israel, for I myself will help you,' declares the LORD, your Redeemer, the Holy One of Israel" (Isaiah 41:9-10, 13-14).

• "Yet this I call to mind and therefore I have hope: Because of the LORD's great love we are not consumed, for his compassions never fail. They are new every morning; great is your faithfulness. I say to myself, 'The LORD is my portion; therefore I will wait for him.' The LORD is good to those whose hope is in him, to the one who seeks him; it is good to wait quietly for the salvation of the LORD" (Lamentations 3:21-26).

• "Come to me, all you who are weary and burdened, and I will give you rest. Take my yoke upon you and learn from me, for I am gentle and humble in heart, and you will find rest for your souls. For my yoke is easy and my burden is light" (Matthew 11:28-30).

• "Keep your lives free from the love of money and be content with what you have, because God has said, 'Never will I leave you; never will I forsake you.' So we say with confidence, 'The Lord is my helper; I will not be afraid. What can man do to me?'" (Hebrews 13:5-6).

Prayer
Heavenly Father, as I look back over my life, I have a choice—to see all the trials and challenges and complain, or to see your constant faithfulness and presence, bow with gratitude, and lift my hands in praise for your goodness. As I look at my present, I also have a choice—to utter a litany of complaints and aches and grumble, or to receive the invitation, "Eat, drink, and be merry," to accept the present with gratitude and joy. Give me grace

to choose gratitude and joy, for my life is under your control. I do trust you. In Jesus' name, Amen.

Chapter Ten

Restoring Peace in Relationships as We Near the Finish Line

I want to begin this chapter with a personal comment. I am including this chapter because of a devastating burden I see when I walk with families in their grief and loss. I realize we are all prone to sin and therefore there will be brokenness and pain in our lives. But my concern is the opinion, regrettably accepted and defended strongly by many people, that they can be in a right relationship with God without concerning themselves with broken relationships they are responsible for or are in. I'll admit that this is not a prominent attitude, yet it concerns me that it exists at all. In this chapter, I want to stress that we should strive to restore relationships in all stages of life, but particularly as we become older.

As we near the finish line of life, we certainly need to be assured that we will cross the finish line and then be in Jesus' presence. Is there anything that will give us a sense of hope, that will allow us to look ahead with assurance that we will be able to celebrate and worship in the home Jesus is preparing for us? We can only have this hope when we are in a right relationship with Jesus. However, as we study the Bible, we learn that being in a right relationship with Jesus means that we will also strive to be in a right relationship with people. Jesus calls us as individuals, but he also calls us to be part of a body and a family.

Some people say that when a person has said a "sinner's prayer," this person is in a right relationship with God and is therefore prepared to cross the finish line. These people will further say that their relationship with God is independent of their relationship with other people. They say, "As long as all is right between me and God, nothing else matters." However, my understanding is that an individual is only fully prepared to cross the finish line when, to the best of this person's ability, her or his relationships are restored and this person is at peace with everyone. We hear Jesus' words, "A new command I give you: Love one another. As I have loved you, so you must love one another. By this all men will know that you are my disciples, if you love one another" (John 13:34-35). This means that a distinct mark of whether we are Jesus' followers is our love.

As we focus on the topic of restoring peace with other people as we near the finish line, two short questions need a clear, definitive answer. The questions are, "Why bother?"

> **A genuine follower of Jesus will**:
> • restore broken relationships
> • love other people
> • strive for peace

and "How?" The first question might be elaborated as: "Why bother restoring peace between myself and others, or between other people, when all that is left of my life is several years, months, or even days?" The second question might be elaborated as: "How can I be expected to have the strength to pursue restoration in relationships when my health is failing, and my energy is limited?"

As you read these words on restoring peace, I am convinced that the matter of restoring relationships is of utmost urgency. I also believe that God will give the necessary strength when there is a dependence on him and a commitment to do all that is necessary to restore relationships. It comes down to the simple question: "Am I willing to do what I can to restore relationships?"

1. Why Bother Restoring Broken Relationships?

I will offer a couple of answers to this question.

a. It Matters to a Holy God.

The ultimate answer is found in the example of God. God bothered to restore humankind to himself. He was so committed to ensure that reconciliation was available that God gave what was most precious to him in order to provide reconciliation for people who were his enemies. In what is possibly the most profound and well-known Bible passage on God's love, we read about how much God gave to restore relationships: "For God so loved the world that he gave his one and only Son, that whoever believes in him shall not perish but have eternal life" (John 3:16). This passage by the Apostle Paul assures us that God not only loved us but that he loved us when we were his enemies: "For if, when we were God's enemies, we were reconciled to him through the death of his Son, how much more, having been reconciled, shall we be saved through his life!" (Romans 5:10). As we place these two passages together, we note that God, the Father of Jesus, gave what was most precious to him, his one and only Son, to reconcile his enemies to himself through the death of his Son.

The answer to the question, "Why bother to restore peace at the end of life?" is that this matters so much to God the Father that he gave what was most precious to him to achieve this reconciliation. God the Father set the example for us. When we genuinely follow Jesus, when we have received the gift of reconciliation, Jesus' complete sacrifice for us, then we will bother to be reconciled with everyone with whom we have a broken relationship.

b. It Matters to Destroyed and Broken People.

A second answer to the question "Why bother to restore a broken relationship?" is that it matters to destroyed and broken people. When a Christian leader has wronged individuals or a Christian father has abused his children, we cannot be silent. We will want to carefully, discreetly, and sensitively speak the truth. By saying nothing, for instance, to a hurting daughter, we are thereby saying that the church, and her God, does not value her. Our words and actions will—by their silence or absence or by carefully chosen words and deeds—address whether we value the dignity and worth of the person who is hurt. May God give us the wisdom and courage to do what is right.

2. How Can I Have the Strength to Pursue Restoration when My Health Is Failing?

The answer to this question is found in the answer to the first question. I will only have the necessary strength when I am rooted in God's sustaining love. This means I must see myself and those with whom I am in conflict as God saw me when he gave his ultimate sacrifice, his only Son. I and whoever I need to pursue reconciliation with are both the objects of God's love—when we were both completely undeserving of his love. Only with God's strength and love can I pursue reconciliation.

Reconciliation and the restoration of relationships is not just a nice topic. This goes to the heart of our God. Therefore, it must go to our hearts as well and move us to action. We must see people as God does—as enemies for whom he gave his best in order to make them his friends. We are called to be reconcilers—on the basis of God's calling and reconciling of us. This must be our priority as we near the finish line of our lives.

"All this is from God, who reconciled us to himself through Christ and gave us the ministry of reconciliation: that God was reconciling the world to himself in Christ, not counting men's sins against them. And he has committed to us the message of reconciliation" (2 Corinthians 5:18-19).

I will briefly note various classes of broken and fractured relationships. Where any of these apply to you, my desire is that the guidelines will give you direction and hope to pursue reconciliation. I believe that the most important legacy any of us can leave is restored and healed relationships. The reverse is therefore also true: the most devastating legacy we can leave is a trail of broken relationships.

3. Preliminary Thoughts on Restoring Relationships

Before I describe the classes of broken and fractured relationships and what is necessary to restore relationships, I want to offer some preliminary thoughts on restoring relationships:

• *The need for sensitivity to hear God's voice.* We might believe that there are no relationships we need to restore. Satan will strive to blind us to broken relationships. David violated Bathsheba, yet was blind to his behavior until the prophet Nathan confronted him and exposed his blindness and sin.

• *The need for an attitude of brokenness.* How easily we justify our innocence in a fractured relationship. We cannot be broken before God and blame and accuse others.

• *The need to keep our focus on God*. This is critical as we consider broken relationships. Satan will want us to focus on the wrong done to us. By focusing on God, we will see as God sees. We will see the other person as God sees him or her (as he or she really is), see ourselves as we really are, and then see a path of restoration to pursue.

• *The need to recognize that we are in a spiritual war.* We are in a war, nothing less. When God's Spirit speaks to us on a specific matter, we must then move forward in obedience and faith, following God's direction.

• *The usefulness of the illustration of three chairs.* A helpful way to understand our responsibility to restore broken relationships is to imagine three chairs—one for the judge, one for an advocate (defense attorney), and one for an accuser (prosecutor). When we sit in the seat of the accuser, we are sitting where the person who has offended us is sitting. When we sit in the seat of the judge, we are taking on the role of a holy and just God. Neither of those seats is ours. We are to sit in the seat of an advocate and, with God's grace and power, seek the welfare of the person who has offended us. (This illustration is taken from material in the seminar, *Whatever It Takes.*)

4. Classes of Broken Relationships

I will now turn to the classes of broken relationships.

a. Restoring Peace when I Have Been Treated Unjustly

Jesus addressed this situation directly: "If your brother sins against you, go and show him his fault, just between the two of you. If he listens to you, you have won your brother over. But if he will not listen, take one or two others along, so that 'every matter may be established by the testimony of two or three witnesses.' If he refuses to listen to them, tell it to the church; and if he refuses to listen even to the church, treat him as you would a pagan or a tax collector" (Matthew 18:15-17).

There is an interesting sidelight to this lesson in the next story in Matthew's Gospel. Peter asked Jesus, "Lord, how many times shall I forgive my brother when he sins against me? Up to seven times?" (Matthew 18:21). We are not given Peter's motive for asking this question. More specifically, why did Peter ask Jesus this question right after Jesus had given clear instructions on how to restore a broken relationship when one person sins against another? Was Peter expressing a forgiving spirit and a commitment to restore a broken relationship? Was Peter willing to follow Jesus' guidelines and forgive a brother up to seven times? There are some possible explanations for Peter's spirit of magnanimity. The teachings of the Jewish scribes and rabbis was that a person should forgive once or twice but a third offence merited no forgiveness. The Babylonian Talmud reads, "When a man sins against another, they forgive him once, they forgive him a second time, they forgive him a third time, but the fourth time they do not forgive him." Peter was expressing a more generous spirit of forgiving than the scribes and rabbis, but his forgiveness still had a limit, albeit higher than the Jewish rabbis. (These clarifications are drawn from Bible commentaries: William Hendriksen, *New Testament Commentary*, Grand Rapids, Michigan: Baker Book House, 1973; Herschel H. Hobbs, *An Exposition of the Gospel of Matthew,* Grand Rapids, Michigan: Baker Book House, 1965; G. Campbell Morgan, *The Gospel according to Matthew*, Old Tappan, New Jersey: Fleming H. Revell Company, 1929.)

However, in Luke's Gospel, Jesus gives us an even more generous path to follow: "If your brother sins, rebuke him and if he repents, forgive him. If he sins against you seven times in a day, and seven times comes back to you, and says, 'I repent,' forgive him" (Luke 17:3-4). This means that forgiveness is to be unlimited.

Recognizing that Matthew 18:15-17 is one of the most practical guidelines Jesus gives on restoring relationships, we need to carefully study what Jesus instructed and then completely follow his directives. Jesus gave four clear steps:

1. "Go and show him his fault, just between the two of you." The goal of this step is to win the brother over.

2. "Take one or two others along." These others, along with the two people who are in a conflict, will do their best to reflect, understand, and listen—again with the goal to "win the brother over." The purpose of recruiting one or two other people is to restore the relationship.

3. "Tell it to the church." Here the conflict is addressed and reconciliation is sought afterward. This implies that the church is entrusted with the ministry of reconciling people within the church.

4. "Treat him as you would a pagan or a tax collector."

Recognizing that this last phrase might be unknown or unfamiliar, I will provide an explanation. What does it mean to treat the person who refuses to listen either to you or to the church as "a pagan or a tax collector?"

May I suggest we find our answer in two avenues: first, by looking at the context, and then, by looking at how Jesus treated pagans and tax collectors.

When we look at the context, we realize that this is the fourth step in attempting to resolve conflict. The first is by one person, the second step is with the assistance of one or two others, and the third step is by the church. All the steps have the goal to bring about reconciliation. If the goal of the first three steps is to move towards the person with the purpose to restore him, then the goal of the fourth step will be the same—to take note of the conflict and then draw the other person back into a restored relationship.

When we consider the example of Jesus, we learn how he treated pagans and tax collectors—he always sought to restore them. A key element of how Jesus treated them is that he ate with them. When we eat with a person, we are committed to be on the same level, to open ourselves to the other person even when we disagree—with the goal to value the person and connect with him or her.

Luke records a story to show how Jesus welcomed and embraced sinners. Tax collectors and sinners gathered around Jesus and wanted to listen to him. Jesus then told three parables to make it perfectly clear how he was treating pagans and tax collectors: first, as a shepherd who sought the one lost sheep until he found it; second, as a woman who swept her house until she found a lost coin; third, as a forgiving father who embraced the prodigal son and restored him into the family. Following each parable is a statement of rejoicing—the first two about the exuberant rejoicing in heaven and the third describing the family celebration over the son who was dead and is alive, who was lost and is found (Luke 15:1-32).

Another story that explains how to treat people as a pagan and a tax collector is in Genesis 3. Immediately after Adam and Eve rejected God and despised his command, he came looking for them (Genesis 3:1-21). To treat a person as a pagan or a tax collector includes both a recognition that the person has estranged/separated himself from us (is lost) and a commitment to draw him back, to look for him until he is found and restored.

There are three further Bible principles regarding restoring relationships in Jesus' teaching in Matthew 18:

1. Our words have authority. In Matthew 18:18, Jesus said, "Whatever you bind on earth will be bound in heaven and whatever you loose on earth will be loosed in heaven."

2. God is present as we reconcile people to ourselves. In Matthew 18:19–20, Jesus said, "Again I tell you that if two of you on earth agree about anything you ask for, it will be done for you by my Father in heaven. For where two or three come together in my name, there am I with them." Normally we quote this passage, especially the last line, "to assure ourselves that God is present, even in the smallest gathering. However, the interpretation from the context eliminates any reference to the small numbers of people gathered. The context means that the number refers to those who come together to seek healing, restoration, and reconciliation. Therefore, the assurance is that God is present especially when two or three witnesses come together in an effort to bring about reconciliation. Reconciliation is of such a high priority that God ensures his presence when people are committed to it. In fact, this is the only place in the Bible where God assures us of his presence when believers gather in a small number. Jesus commits to be present with us when we take seriously the mission of reconciliation because this is his mission. We are on holy ground—with God's presence among us—as we seek to do his mission, bringing peace where there is conflict and healing where there is disease.

3. Be lavish in forgiving. Peter heard Jesus teach that reconciliation and forgiveness is a core practice for believers. Then he followed up the teaching with the valid and relevant question, "Lord, how many times shall I forgive my brother when he sins against me? Up to seven times?" (Matthew 18:21). We don't know what prompted Peter's question. Was he simply wanting information? Or did he want to present himself as a very forgiving person? Jesus' response referred back to Lamech, who bragged to his two wives, "Adah and Zillah, listen to me; wives of Lamech, hear my words. I have killed a man for wounding me, a young man for injuring me. If Cain is avenged seven times, then Lamech seventy-seven times"

(Genesis 4:23-24). Jesus' answer to Peter's question about forgiveness is a counterpart to Lamech's vicious announcement of personal revenge. Even as Lamech announced ferocious, brutal, and multiplied personal revenge, so Jesus instructed equal, if not greater, personal forgiveness. As Lamech was committed to repeated vicious revenge, so we who follow Christ should be committed to lavish and generous forgiveness.

b. *Restoring Peace* when People Believe They *Have Been Treated Unjustly*

When a person believes he or she has been wronged, this conclusion might be drawn from inaccurate or partial information. Or their information might be accurate, but their conclusion distorted. Either way, they hurt, and their understanding is darkened. They judge by assumption, appearance, and hearsay. They see themselves as victims and not responsible for their responses, for their part in a broken relationship, for their actions, for their perceptions, or for their duty to restore the relationship. Proverbs 18:19 says, "An offended brother is more unyielding than a fortified city, and disputes are like the barred gates of a citadel."

I don't have any quick and easy answer or formula to explain how to follow Jesus' way to restore peace when a person believes he or she has been treated unjustly. However, may I offer some direction in this difficult subject:

i. If you are uncertain about what actually happened, wait and check your own heart first. I confess I have not always done this. However, as I have checked my own heart, I have often sensed God's Spirit directing me to leave the situation in his hands. I found this instruction to be helpful: "It is mine to avenge; I will repay....The LORD will judge his people and have compassion on his servants" (Deuteronomy 32:35–36).

ii. God promises that he will maintain justice and avenge when necessary. Both the Apostle Paul and the author of Hebrews point to this truth (Romans 12:17-21, Hebrews 10:30-31). I take assurance that the passage in Deuteronomy brings together two commitments on God's part. First, he will avenge and do as he sees fit. Second, he will have compassion on his servants. We rest in the assurance that God is not only fair but is also compassionate.

iii. Seek God's help. The Psalmist's prayer is a helpful corrective: "Search me, O God, and know my heart; test me and know my anxious thoughts. See if there is any offensive way in me, and lead me in the way everlasting" (Psalm 139:23-24).

iv. Take responsibility. A verse that speaks directly to what might be happening in the soil of my heart when I am offended or believe I am offended (believe I have been treated unjustly) is: "Make every effort to live in peace with all men and to be holy; without holiness no one will see the Lord. See to it that no one misses the grace of God and that no bitter root grows up to cause trouble and defile many" (Hebrews 12:14-15). This verse implies that I am responsible for the soil of my heart, and since this is the case, when bitterness is growing, then I need to search my heart.

v. Don't be hasty. Is it necessary to speak to a person who I believe has offended me? Maybe I'm just timid when I suggest that we should lean towards hesitation before taking action. My hesitancy is based on these two factors. First, I want to follow Jesus' instructions when there are clear offences (Matthew 18:15-17). Second, I want to search my own heart, check the condition of the soil of my heart, give the concern to God, and extend grace. Since we live in a fallen world, we will offend and be offended constantly. Then there will be times when we are not certain whether either has happened. Possibly the best approach is to leave these uncertain times to God and check the soil in our hearts. Even better, we should till into our soil the character qualities in the Beatitudes, beginning with "Blessed are the merciful." I am in enormous need of mercy—may I extend it in equal abundance.

c. Restoring Peace when I Have Treated Another Person Unjustly

The matter of maintaining right relationships and restoring broken relationships is a core element in the Christian faith. This is much more than a responsibility or commandment for those who claim to follow Jesus. The very *essence* of the Christian message is reconciliation and restored relationships. The centrality of right relationships is based on who our God is and on the unity within the Trinity. Jesus' prayer is that the unity between him and his Father would also be between himself and his followers and *among* his followers (John 17:11, 20-24).

Further, we will not be able to worship God when we have a broken relationship with another person. Jesus taught the seriousness of offences when he said, "If you are offering your gift at the altar and there remember that your brother has something against you, leave your gift there in front of the altar. First go and be reconciled to your brother; then come and offer your gift. Settle matters quickly with your adversary who is taking you to court" (Matthew 5:23-25).

The seriousness of mending relationships was also stressed by the Apostle Paul when he wrote, "If it is possible, as much as depends on you, live at peace with everyone" (Romans 12:18).

How do we approach people we have offended? To make this more personal, I will change the question into the singular: How do I approach a person I have offended? I must begin the journey of reconciliation as one who has been reconciled and whose very nature is birthed and based in a God whose nature is one of peace and making peace. Therefore, I will come with humility, dependence on God, and vulnerability, not demanding anything.

• I always begin with the premise that I am responsible for what I have done, never trying to give any explanations or justifications.

• I will not seek to justify or explain my motives. Even if the other person says that I am selfish, inconsiderate, proud, rude, harsh, and arrogant and states this is the reason I am seeking reconciliation, I will only assure the person of my responsibility for my actions and attitude and my desire for reconciliation.

• I will not insist that I am right, thereby implying the other person is wrong.

• Instead, I will listen. I will seek both to hear and then to understand the other person. I will hear how this person understands my words and senses my motives. I will remain silent until the person has said all that he wants to say. Even then I will ask, "Do I understand this is what you are saying?" If I don't agree with the other person's understanding of what I said or did, the key is to respect this. Then, I will request that he forgives me for offending him. I will commit to search my motives and leave the relationship in God's hand.

> **Our Intentions, Their Actions**
> Often we judge ourselves by our intentions and judge everyone else by their actions. (John Bevere, *Bait of Satan*, 243.)

• I will never say, "If I have offended you, please forgive me." The bottom line of this statement is: "It is your fault that you are offended. I never meant to offend you, and since you are offended, that is your problem."

• I will say, "Where I have wronged you, please forgive me."

Following these steps is among the hardest things we can ever do or say. But, when we genuinely follow our God, who reconciled the world through the death of his Son, then we will take any action required to seek reconciliation. Restoring peace is at the heart of God. May this also be at the core of our heart.

d. Restoring Peace when There Is Discord between Other People

Our goal of reconciliation applies not only for ourselves but also for other people. Sometimes we are aware of a conflict between people and one or both of these people is becoming weaker and may only have a limited number of months or even days left. This becomes more critical and personal when there is conflict between members of our own family. Do we simply let it be, or do we get down on our knees, pray for godly wisdom, grace, and courage, and then take the bold step to urge those family members who are in conflict to restore their relationship?

One evidence that we are genuine followers of Jesus is that we will be peacemakers, as is manifest in Jesus' Beatitude: "Blessed are the peacemakers, for they will be called sons of God" (Matthew 5:9). Are we tempted to see the struggles in our neighborhoods, our cities, and even our world and respond, "During my life, I have been involved in many things, but now, in retirement and towards the end of life, I need to let others be involved. My time was then, not anymore"? As we become frail and struggle with a lot of pain, do we have a sense that we should withdraw from our involvements? We might rationalize it this way: "What can I do, now that I am old and feeble? Why should I concern myself with the issues around me?"

The answer to these questions is that, as followers of Jesus, we have his nature, and we will therefore seek to be peacemakers, no matter what age we are or even how frail we are. Actually, our life experiences should have sensitized us so that we are more capable to be reconcilers and peacemakers now than when we were younger and possibly more impulsive and demanding. May God give us courage to become involved and engaged in the ministry of reconciliation. This is at the core of who we are.

> Is it possible to approach this matter from another vantage point? Imagine that we have had a difficult and broken relationship with someone for many years and have an inner longing to be restored. But we are becoming weaker and do not know how to begin the process of reconciliation. Would we not wish that a peacemaker would help us to restore the relationship?

e. Restoring Peace with Those Who Have Died

This applies when those who have offended us have died, as well as when we have offended someone and this person has died. The sobering reality is that this happens all too frequently. How do we find an answer and restoration—or is this not possible?

We know that the person who has offended us and is now dead will not come and ask for forgiveness. Does this mean we need to live with bitterness? Also, we know that when we have offended someone and this person has passed away, we likewise cannot seek forgiveness from him. Does this mean we need to live with regret? To varying degrees both scenarios are present with each of us. The reason is that we are continuously offending and being offended against.

An answer regarding the matter of restoring peace with those who have died involves a discussion on the topic of forgiveness. I believe that reconciliation is critical all the time, but there is a degree of urgency when we are placing this concern in the context of the final stages of life. (In the Appendix, there is a short list of books on reconciliation and forgiveness.)

I see reconciliation as part of a healing process. This healing process involves the following elements: confession, forgiveness, reconciliation, and then healing. The ideal is that all four of these elements will happen. When a wrong has occurred, a person will confess his wrong, the confession will be accepted, and forgiveness will be extended. This results in a reconciliation of the two parties, and then healing can begin. The critical question when we are speaking to the issue of restoring peace with those who have died is: "Can there be forgiveness when there is no confession?" We know the ideal is that all four elements will be included, but a dead person cannot confess. Nor can we confess to a dead person.

May I suggest that our answer is in Jesus' example. On the cross, he declared, "Father, forgive them, for they do not know what they are doing" (Luke 23:34). As we follow the crucifixion story, we see that the people he was referring to had not confessed what they were doing, nor were they reconciled. If Jesus had waited until his enemies felt some guilt or shame for their words or actions, he would never have forgiven them. Jesus' example demonstrates that total forgiveness must take place in the heart. If I have a genuine heart experience of forgiveness, I will not be devastated if there is no reconciliation. If those who hurt me don't want to be reconciled and be in a mended relationship with me, it isn't my problem because I have forgiven them and released them. I will feel hurt and wish it was otherwise, but I will have released them in my heart.

I believe this is how we can find an answer regarding someone who has offended us and has died. With this understanding of forgiveness, a person can achieve inner peace even when forgiving someone who has died. This person cannot confess to us, but we can still forgive, we can still free that person from what they did against us. This also applies in a situation where a person who is still living refuses to confess. The same principle applies. It is also then in our power and it is our responsibility to forgive.

The above explanation speaks to the situation where a person who has offended us has died. I have the ability and responsibility to forgive him and thereby release him of any wrong he has done to me. But what about the situation where I have offended a person who has died? The Holy Spirit convicts me of the wrong I have done, but I cannot go to this person and confess my wrong. Do I live with this turmoil and guilt in my heart?

I believe an answer can be found when we consider the core essence of sin. Sin, wickedness, and iniquity are first and foremost attitudes and actions against God. Our sinful attitude towards God is demonstrated in wrong and destructive behavior towards people. David understood this when he confessed, "*Against you, you only*, have I sinned and done what is evil in your sight, so that you are proved right when you speak and justified when you judge" (Psalm 51:4, emphasis added). When the prophet Nathan confronted David of the sin of adultery, David confessed to Nathan, "I have sinned against the LORD" (2 Samuel 12:13).

There are several other stories that reinforce this understanding that sin is primarily against God:

• When Abraham and Sarah moved into the region of Gerar, Abimelech, the king of Gerar, took Sarah. God spoke to Abimelech in a dream, saying, "I know you did this with a clear conscience, and so I have kept you from sinning *against me*" (Genesis 20:6, emphasis added).

• Joseph was responsible for Potiphar's household. When Potiphar's wife made an immoral advance on Joseph, he responded, "How then could I do such a wicked thing and sin *against God?*" (Genesis 39:6-10, emphasis added).

• When the prodigal son came to his senses he formulated his confession, which included these words: "Father, I have sinned *against heaven* and against you" (Luke 15:17-21, emphasis added).

With the understanding that sin at its core is a heart attitude towards God that is demonstrated in behavior towards people, I see a way forward when I know that I have offended a person who is now dead. Instead of going to that person who is dead (which I cannot do), I can and will go to God, confess my sin, and ask for forgiveness. Here, as in all incidents of sin, the instruction given by the Apostle John applies: "If we confess our sins, he is faithful and just and will forgive us our sins and purify us from all unrighteousness" (1 John 1:9).

5. Restoring Peace within the Family

I have presented five classes of broken relationships and have provided a brief direction to help restore peace in each area. In actual fact, all five of these classes of broken relationships are demonstrated in families. This becomes evident when families come to plan a funeral service for their loved ones. There is a phenomenal contrast between walking with a family where I have sensed the beloved mother or father was committed to having positive relationships and being at peace with all people within the family and beyond, and walking with a family where there was discord, animosity, and division. I believe the topic of restoring peace within the family deserves special attention, and therefore I will focus specifically on this critical issue in this separate section. Having said this, the principles in the first five classes apply to the family as well.

I will begin the discussion of restoring peace within the family with several questions. I invite you to ask these of yourself:

1. When I look at my family—my uncles and aunts, my brothers and sisters—is there a sense of unity and harmony or a sense of conflict and avoidance? Or were there other ways we related?

2. When I look back at my family experience when I was a child and young person, was there joy and grace or fear and criticism, or were there other emotions within my family?

3. From my parents, did I sense affirmation and blessings or judgement and put downs? Were there any other feelings?

4. Can I think about or talk about how serious I feel about having all my relationships mended within my family?

5. Why is it necessary or important to attempt to restore relationships?

6. What legacy do I wish to give my children?

7. How have I attempted to bring about peace within my family?

8. How do I respond when I observe character flaws and sinful behavior in my children that I observed were in my parents? Do I respond with anger, fear, repentance, or some other reaction?

a. The Nature of Forgiveness

The matter of broken relationships within a family is so very "close to home"—it is actually at home—that it is difficult to face these issues and respond in a wise and effective manner. Often parents deal with broken relationships in their family of origin by modeling the same brokenness—and their children learn to deal with brokenness in the same way as they were taught. Then, this behavior will continue from generation to generation unless a new approach is taken. To break this destructive mode of family relationships, it is necessary to recognize it for what it is. It is impossible to fully explain this in a short space, but I wish to point to some ways that I trust will bring about reconciliation and peace within a family.

i. Forgive or Excuse

We begin with the two approaches to deal with family discord: forgiving or excusing. This image helps me understand what is necessary to bring peace within a family. Imagine the family you are in now as a room filled with discord, fear, non-affirmation, a judgmental spirit, and even abuse and violence. You desperately want out of this room. You see two doors. One is marked "Confess and Forgive," and the second is marked "Excuse." The only door that will break the generational curse is the door marked "Confess and Forgive." If a family member walks through the door marked "Excuse," this person will step into an identical room of broken relationships.

ii. Confess and Forgive

Making a decision to forgive and actually forgiving are two different things. Forgiveness must be grounded in truth. We can only forgive to the degree that we know the extent of the damage inflicted. We will not forgive when we minimize, deny, or ignore the damage done. To forgive, we first need to feel the pain of the wound and know the consequence of the injury.

iii. Forgive

Forgiveness means to first, recognize the extent of the damage done to us, and second, hand over to God the right to stand in judgment.

iv. Excuse

To excuse is to overlook and make allowances for bad behavior. When we excuse, we take the focus from where it belongs, on the transgressor, and place it somewhere else. For example, we can take the focus away from the transgressor and place it on our society or on our family history or even on ourselves, the victim. Here we, as children, take the blame for our parents' violence.

Here are some excuses offered for parental malpractice:
• My parents really had a hard time growing up.
• They did the best they could.
• They were really struggling when I was a child.
• My dad spent long hours at work trying to help the family survive.
• Trying to avoid the mistakes of their own parents, they swung too far the opposite way.
• Worrying about money made them angry, but they were trying to make our life better than the one they had.
• They did not know any better.
• They were sickly.
• It was the culture that shaped them.
• It will not do any good to stir this up.
• I can cope with my parents' shortcomings.
• In many ways, he was a good father.
• My parents didn't become Christians until later.
• If they knew the impact of their sin on me, it would destroy them.
• It's okay because I have broad shoulders and I can carry it.
• It's no big deal because I am not worth it anyway.
(Trevor Walters, *EAS Syndrome*, 80-81.)

b. Giving and Receiving a Blessing

A related issue to broken relationships within a family is "blessing." This is not a separate and unconnected issue. The way God has designed a family is that parents are to be the avenue through which God extends his blessings, pouring them onto the children within the family.

The example of God, the Father, will demonstrate and help to explain this. After Jesus' baptism we read, "He saw heaven being torn open and the Spirit descending on him like a dove. And a voice came from heaven: 'You are my Son, whom I love; with you I am well pleased'" (Mark 1:10-11). Trevor Walters explains: "Jesus' Father's blessing enveloped Jesus before Jesus could ever have done anything to earn it....His Father's blessing was totally grace-based. It wasn't in the least dependent on any past achievement or any expectation of future performance" (Trevor Walters, *EAS Syndrome*, 20).

Where is the connection between "blessing" and resolving family brokenness? We begin with the plan God has for parents, especially fathers. Generally, children draw their perception of God, the Father, from their earthly father. God has designed it that children are to be blessed—affirmed for who they are, not because of what they have done or what they might do in the future—and this blessing will come primarily through the father.

How does a father pass on God's blessing to his children? The father will first need to receive the blessing of the heavenly Father. Using the image of soil, the father will need to have soft and rich soil so that God's Spirit will produce the fruit of the Spirit. The father's fruit of the Spirit (described by the Apostle Paul in Galatians 5:22-26) will be received by a child as a blessing and an affirmation. Paul's description of the fruit of the Spirit is followed by a brief comment that applies to the matter of family unity or discord. A father will either live in such a manner that his life will show the fruit of the Spirit, or his life will exhibit the deeds of the sinful nature. A child will feel the father's blessings, as evidenced by the fruit of the Spirit, or the father's lack of affirmation, as evidenced by the three final actions listed by Paul: being conceited, provoking, and envying.

c. Sour Grapes or Delicious Fruit?

At times, we might believe a family's dysfunction and brokenness is so major that it is futile to attempt to work towards any resolution. We cannot see any change possible. We despair that the brokenness that has been handed down through generations will continue like a mighty waterfall for the next many generations. We might even refer to the biblical proverb: "The fathers have eaten sour grapes and the children's teeth are set on edge" (Jeremiah 31:29, expanded and interpreted in

Page | 114

Ezekiel 18:1-32). The Israelites used this proverb as a form of self-pity, fatalism, and despair. They claimed that they were not responsible for their own behavior and that any ill effect on themselves was inevitable. They based this claim on a false interpretation and application of Exodus 20:5 and Numbers 14:18. There it states that a man's sins can have a negative effect on his descendants. However, this does not take away from the fact that every person is responsible for his own behavior. Ezekiel's teaching on this topic concludes with, "For I take no pleasure in the death of anyone, declares the Sovereign LORD. Repent and live!" (Ezekiel 18:32). The application for our topic—resolving division within the family—is that our gracious God calls us to repentance and to new life. Then the father and family will produce, not sour grapes, but delicious fruit for their children and grandchildren.

Reflection #1
Why is it that so many families, even Christian families, not only have significant divisions among their various members, but that there seems to be no urgency among them to restore relationships even as individuals come to the last months of life?

Reflection #2
Do I feel an urgency to restore a broken relationship—whether this is between myself and someone else or between two other people?

If so, what will I base reconciliation on? Do I really believe that God, through Jesus, has given me the ministry of reconciliation?

How will I commit to restoring relationships:
• with those who have done me wrong?
• with those I have wronged?
• with those who have died?
• among other people when I sense discord among family members?

How will I do what I can to restore friendship and peace?

Prayer:
Heavenly Father, this chapter has been difficult. As I look back, I wish that things had been different. There was pain, a spirit of fear—certainly not affirmation—in the family in which I grew up. I did not feel blessed or valued for who I was. Today I look up to you, seeking your affirmation and love, but also seeking the necessary courage to make wise decisions. I know I will need help. May I reach out, accepting the help I need so that your blessings will flow in me and then through me to my children and through them to my grandchildren. May I hear your reassuring words, "You are my child, whom I love; with you I am well pleased." May I then

say the same to my children, with your power and grace. In Jesus' name, Amen.

Chapter Eleven
Running the Race and Crossing the Finish Line in Community

We have heard the proverb, "It takes a village to raise a child." Society will rally around a newborn child and support the parents. The grandmother will come, often from a long distance, and give needed help, even when there is a normal birth and the child is healthy. In some societies, a mother is expected to bring her newborn child and move back to her parents' and grandparents' neighborhood. The extended family will then be involved in the care and the upbringing of the child.

We also recognize the need to have a stable home for teenagers. When a home is dysfunctional, the child is moved into a foster home, according to government guidelines that seek to provide the best possible environment for children and teenagers.

And, when a man and woman commit themselves to one another for life in marriage, the families and friends will again gather to give their support and blessing.

These three examples demonstrate that a common feature in any stable society is a strong interconnectedness among the citizens. In such a society, all members watch out for each other. This sense of community will be evident across generations, so that children feel loved by their grandparents and youth are considerate of the elderly. The members of such a society lean into each other, instead of distancing themselves. They embrace each other instead of turning away from one another. A society in which individuals are isolated or feel shunned and marginalized will disintegrate.

As we return to the metaphor of a marathon, I want to add another element. This element is that every runner needs the help of other people in order to successfully cross the finish line. Before a runner enters a marathon, she will consult a trainer or medical person to ensure she is in proper physical condition to be able to complete the long marathon. Individuals will prepare the track so that it will be safe for the runners. Along the marathon path will be medical stations, as well as people who have fresh water for the runners. These support systems are more frequent and critical the closer a runner approaches the finish line.

The application to the subject of preparing to cross the finish line in life is this: as in a marathon where a runner needs other people, so each one of us needs support and help throughout the various stages of our life. But this help is most critical when we become frail and vulnerable towards the end of our lives, as we strain to run the last lap of the marathon of life.

The emphasis throughout this book is that each person is responsible to be prepared to cross the finish line. However, it is necessary to add another emphasis—on the significance and responsibility of the community in helping to ensure that we will successfully cross the finish line. The sober reality is that we cannot finish well on our own. We need one another.

There are several principles that are crucial if the elderly are to be cared for in a healthy and supportive community and are able to cross their finish line with hope, courage, the necessary strength, and the endurance they will need.

1. An Acknowledgement that We Live in an Individualistic Society

Various sayings point out our Western society's spirit of individualistic pride, including "If it is to be, it's up to me" and "I did it my way." In a memorial service, we may hear words of acclamation such as "What an accomplishment," "He did it all by himself," and "He certainly had many achievements and successes." When individuals are in their youth or young adulthood, they might believe they can make it on their own. Our Western society promotes individualism, admires self-made, independent people, and places on a pedestal those who seemed to make it on their own. Yet at no stage in life is a person ever independent.

This spirit of individualism is of particular significance as a person becomes older. Earlier in life, when a person was stronger, he might have assumed he was self-sufficient and did not need anyone else. But when a person becomes older and weaker, the myth of being independent needs to be acknowledged for what it is—a myth and a falsehood. Yet, how often older men and women want to assume they can function alone without any support. This is unrealistic, and it puts unnecessary stress on their families and close friends.

When a person becomes weaker in advancing years, a difficult balance or tension needs to be faced. This tension is between giving a person control over his own decisions and confronting him when he is unrealistic in what he believes he can do. His spirit of independence needs to be addressed, faced, and even challenged.

2. Weep with Those who Weep

After a memorial service, a friend of the family approached me and said, "What is wrong with all of us? No one cried. No one showed any emotions. Did no one love our dear friend? Did none of the family members really love their mother and grandmother?"

Christians in Western churches will certainly not be accused of wailing, tearing their clothes, and throwing dust and ashes into the air, which are common expressions of grief in some other cultures. But have we drifted too far to the other extreme? If we genuinely love our mother, or whomever we are conducting the funeral service for, and know that we will never again see her on earth, then this should be evident in our deep sorrow.

I recall hearing the testimony of a widow whose husband was murdered while they were missionaries. At that time, I was just beginning my pastoral ministry, having conducted only one or two funerals. But I sensed something was not fitting as I listened to her testimony. This widow had been asked to be a key speaker in our church's missions event. Instead of an expression of deep grief over the murder of her husband, she only talked of how God was with her. Certainly, I rejoiced that God was with her and that she felt God's presence and compassion in the tragic murder of her husband. But why did she, a Christian leader, not even hint at the loss and the grief I expected her to be experiencing—not only over losing her husband but also over having to relinquish the vision of being a missionary with him? Why did she need to be silent about her pain? Did she have any feelings of anger and frustration, or even doubt about God's ways? Why did it seem that the whole congregation, except for me, did not see that something was not authentic? Those were the questions I felt in my heart.

The words written by the preacher in Ecclesiastes 3:1-8 are regularly spoken at funeral services. They begin, "There is a time for everything, and a season for every activity under heaven." Then the preacher lists a series of "opposites." The two opposites that apply to a funeral service are "weeping and laughing" and "mourning and dancing." I cannot go into detail on the subject of grief, loss, and mourning—this would require more space than I have here. But I have experienced how this passage has been misinterpreted and misused so that grieving people have been left without hope and without comfort.

First, this text can be used in such a way as to leave grieving people with no hope. The text can be seen to mean that we have little or no capacity to change the situations that happen to us and to others. The interpretation is that God's timing is perfect and therefore we are not to interfere. This interpretation includes the premise that sometimes God provides painful occasions for weeping and mourning and at other times he gives us pleasant experiences for laughing and dancing. In my opinion, this is an improper reading of the text. The message of the whole book of Ecclesiastes, including the words on the opposites that life presents, is that God is infinitely concerned for the world but is also sovereign. Life is made up of both of these contrasts. These are givens. The preacher is not thereby implying that both are good, merely that both just *are*. Furthermore, the book teaches that when good or bad, painful or pleasant experiences happen, God is still in control. Therefore, we are called to trust God and submit to him, as expressed in the final words of the book, "Here is the conclusion of the matter: Fear God and keep his commandments, for this is the whole duty of man" (Ecclesiastes 12:13). Applying this specifically to valleys of pain, grief, and loss, the message is that we can trust God—even when we do not understand and cannot make sense of our tragedy. As we hold on to God in our grief, we believe he walks with us in our valley of death. This gives us hope, knowing God is present even—and especially—in the darkest valley of absolute loss and uncontrolled grief.

The passage in Ecclesiastes that lists the opposites has also been misused in another manner that leaves people without comfort. I recall a phone call from a close friend of a grieving widow. The caller requested that I visit this widow, whose husband had passed away several years earlier. The reason this close friend wanted me to go to the widow and speak to her was, "She has grieved long enough. She needs to get over it and get on with life." This friend thought that I, as the pastor, could coerce this widow to cease grieving. Possibly the friend of this widow had heard some preacher read Ecclesiastes 3:1-8 and then admonish the audience, "People, there was a time to weep and a time to mourn. But that time is long past. Now is a time to laugh and to dance." Some preachers even go so far as to point to admonitions such as, "Be joyful always, pray continually; give thanks in all circumstances" (1 Thessalonians 5:16-18) and then tell people that they should not grieve or weep. This is an absolute misuse of Scripture. It insults those who are grieving and shows an ignorance of human nature.

Jesus' words apply here: "Blessed are those who mourn, for they will be comforted" (Matthew 5:4). Jesus did not promise, "Blessed are those who refrain from mourning." Keeping a stiff upper lip in a time of sorrow and forcing ourselves not to break down when sharing a tribute to a dear mother might be good stoicism, but it is certainly not good Christianity. God created us with the full range of emotions, and we are meant to experience them all. Jesus promised, "The thief comes only to steal and kill and destroy; I have come that they may have life and have it to the full" (John 10:10). But how do we apply that verse? Have we defined the "life to the full" that Jesus came to give as a life in which all our wants are met and we feel pleasant and joyful all the time? A study of the 150 Psalms shows that the largest group of psalms are lament psalms. In these lament psalms, the Psalmist cried out to the Lord, trusting in the Lord's constant presence, goodness, and power. The Psalmist believed that the Lord is always present and that he will hear and will answer. I believe we will readily agree that the Psalmists who expressed these laments had a deep trust in the Lord. The Psalmists who lamented and cried out to the Lord lived life to the full, even in their distress and loss. Therefore, we can state that the full life that Jesus has come to give will include extreme grief.

Family, it is right that you express grief and sorrow, even to the point of sobbing and being unable to continue speaking when you share deeply about a dear mother. I remember several times that the following would happen. A family member, usually a son, would share a moving tribute about his mother. Then he would come to me after the service and say, "I was so afraid that I would begin sobbing and just bawl like a little baby. I am so glad I was able to control myself." How I wished that this son did not feel such pressure to remain calm. I wish that son had known that when he grieved, he could let it show.

Jesus wept with the two sisters Mary and Martha at the death of their brother Lazarus. Paul described God as "the Father of compassion and the God of all comfort, who comforts us in all our troubles, so that we can comfort those in any trouble with the comfort we ourselves have received from God" (2 Corinthians 1:3). Our grief is an expression of our emotions, demonstrating that we have lost someone who is precious.

I have expanded on the aspect of "weeping with those who weep" because I believe it is an important reminder, particularly in our Western society where we attempt to control our grief.

Another reason I have expanded on the need to "weep with those who weep" is because this applies particularly to older adults. As a person reaches the last years of her life, she will have an accumulation of loss after loss. These are only some of them: the loss of children as they left home, the loss of a career, the loss of health, the loss of dignity if the bodily functions cannot be controlled, the loss of a spouse, the loss of friends. Therefore, it is critical that family and friends will support this elderly person. May we never express thoughts such as, "I know what it is like, and I understand you." May none of us hesitate to sit with those who are grieving. May we let them bawl, even uncontrollably. May we simply be present—just sit and listen, and maybe just sit.

3. The Balance between Supporting and Empowering/Resourcing

We need to empower and resource people so that they are prepared to run the final part of their marathon of life and successfully cross the finish line. We also need to recognize that their community—their family and close friends—will have a major bearing on their failure or success in their last years.

The Apostle Paul pointed to the balance between supporting and empowering when he instructed Christians to "carry each other's burden, and in this way you will fulfill the law of Christ" and also taught, "Each one should carry his own load" (Galatians 6:2, 5). In other words, the community, the church, and the family are responsible to support the elderly people in their midst. At the same time, these elderly people are responsible for doing what they can do.

The following is an example of this balance. We encourage individuals to plan ahead and make certain their pension plans and medical insurance will sustain them in their final years. However, we must admit that many people who have been living under the poverty line all their lives have not been able to put aside savings for their retirement, much less the years when they need major medical care. This means that we, as members of a church, will think of those who are frail in their final years. As citizens in our country, we need to speak up and advocate that scarce resources will be allocated to help the frail elderly.

4. A Society's Care for the Weak and Vulnerable

It is well documented that a society can be measured by how it treats those members who are frail and weak. This also applies to a religion and a value system. The Apostle James defined the essence of pure religion with these words: "Religion that God our Father accepts as pure and faultless is this: to look after orphans and widows in their distress and to keep oneself from being polluted by the world" (James 1:27). Jesus stressed the importance of caring for those in need, noting that when we do so, we are in fact doing this for him: "Whatever you did for one of the least of these brothers of mine, you did for me" (Matthew 25:31-40). We, who claim to follow Jesus, will want to commit our time, examine our priorities, reallocate our resources, and advocate that the frail and elderly will be cared for.

In the Jewish culture of the first century, the oldest son was responsible for the care of his mother if his father had passed away. We are familiar with Jesus' sensitive and compassionate words, spoken when he was suffering unimaginable pain and loss as he was hanging on the cross. To his mother Jesus said, "Dear woman, here is your son." To the beloved disciple John he said, "Here is your mother" (John 19:26-27). With those words, John was given responsibility for Jesus' mother. We know that at the time of Jesus' crucifixion, his brothers did not believe in him even though they were among the believers after Jesus' ascension (John 7:5, Acts1:14).

As those who follow Jesus, we need to accept our responsibility to care for our elderly, not only within our churches, but also within our neighborhoods and cities. In summary, caring for, walking with, and being present with the weak and vulnerable in the last years of their lives is at the core of our Christian faith. May the way we fulfill this responsibility be compelling evidence of our faith in God.

5. The Various Models of Living in Community

Care for our frail elderly is a key component of a stable and whole society. There are various models of how we can provide a caring environment for our elderly. For most of society's history, frail seniors were cared for within their own families and in the community. This is still the practice in many Eastern cultures. A fairly recent phenomenon is the building of care homes for the elderly. These care homes often have several levels of support—from minimal assistance through partial support to full support.

However, a harsh reality, at least in our Canadian society, is that there are not enough financial resources to build care homes for all of our seniors, even if we agreed that this is the best way to care for our elderly. Also, the villages or communities for seniors offering the various levels of care are limited to only a small segment of our society who can afford this avenue of care. Having noted this, our Canadian health system provides subsidized complex care for the individuals with the greatest need. However, there are several major issues involved.

• Awareness of the available care resources needs greater attention. Elderly people, along with their families, need clear directions on how to "navigate the health care system." All too often, older adults and their families do not know how to take the next steps—from living at home to receiving support at home to independent living in a seniors' facility and then to the various levels of complex care.

• Individuals with limited financial resources have challenges navigating the transitions from being fully independent to needing full care.

• The models of support should be appropriate to the people involved. In other words, what might fit some cultural groups will not fit other groups. We will want to ensure that every senior is cared for in a way that is most desirable to her or him, even though the model of care will vary.

6. Are We Our Elders' Keepers?

After Cain, in a spirit of jealousy and anger, killed his brother Abel, God confronted Cain with the question, "Where is your brother Abel?" We know the callous response by Cain: "I don't know. Am I my brother's keeper?" (Genesis 4:1-12). As families, as neighborhoods, as church congregations, and as citizens of our country, we have a responsibility to know where our elderly people are and what their needs are. This means we need to listen to them, sit with them, and hear what they desire. We are our elders' keepers.

I recall a conversation about the ministries churches were providing for seniors. A denominational leader and pastor gave this comment, "Our focus and energy is on the next generation—on the children and youth. The seniors are capable of caring for themselves, and therefore the church should not provide any ministry for them." Regrettably, this attitude is very familiar and widely accepted among Western evangelical churches.

Another example is a senior pastor of a church who characterized his seniors as being in the categories: no go, slow go, and fast go. Those categorized as "no go" tended to be frail, demented, and dependent upon others, while those categorized as "fast go" were strong and independent. Those who were characterized as "slow go" were somewhere in between. James M. Houston and Michael Parker responded to this regrettable caricature of our elders with, "The church should ask the hard question: what value to society is a 'no go'?" And they say we should answer confidently: "An incontinent, dependent person suffering from late-stage Alzheimer's disease provides the person's family and church with one of life's most important lessons. This is an opportunity to learn how to love a person unconditionally, without any expectation of something in return."

If the church continues to relegate its responsibilities toward its senior members to other institutions in society and fails to recognize the gifts that lie within those members, it will become like salt that has lost its taste, its purpose, and its capacity to preserve that which is good, and it will have lost its capacity to light the way. Houston and Parker conclude: "The aging church is not an accident. It is God himself who has granted longer life for his purposes, and we believe that elders hold the keys to solving many, if not most, of society's problems" (Houston and Parker, *A Vision for the Aging Church*, 31-33).

The early church recognized its responsibility to care for the frail elderly. Here are three examples of how the early church cared for dependent and weak seniors:
• Specific steps were taken by the Twelve to ensure that widows from the Grecian Jews would receive daily food (Acts 6:1-7).
• The Apostle Paul instructed Timothy to "Give proper recognition to those widows who are really in need" (1 Timothy 5:3).
• James, the brother of Jesus, described the religion that God our Father accepts as pure and faultless is one that "looks after orphans and widows in their distress" (James 1:27).

In summary, we, as families, as churches, and as a society, are our elders' keepers, especially as they near the finish line of their lives.

7. Mentoring: Valuing the Wisdom and Blessings of Our Elderly

The first six sections of this chapter discussed various expressions of walking with and caring for the elderly. In various degrees, these sections described what the family, the church, and society should do for the elderly.

This seventh section replaces what we do "to" and "for" the elderly with what is done "with" or "by" the elderly, what we receive "from" the elderly. Regrettably, there is a pervasive belief that seniors are a group that need help and that ministries and services should be directed "to" and "for" them. This view is prominent within most Western congregations and government agencies. Yet possibly one of the greatest gifts that can be bestowed on our elderly people is welcoming the gifts that they can bestow on the rest of society. However, little effort is made in the areas of consulting them, seeking their advice, working with them, affirming them, appreciating them, and requesting what they can provide.

In the last lap of a marathon race, the runner's focus and energy are directed towards completing the marathon. But, in the marathon of life, God has so designed society that that those in the last lap have more to do than simply ensuring that they themselves make it across the finish line. God has so designed us that we will want to help other people in life. This is the reason he has placed us within families and in communities. Possibly one of the greatest things that will motivate our elderly people is if we acknowledge their worth. Their value is a given, but it is often not affirmed nor appreciated.

The Apostle Paul unashamedly instructed the Corinthian believers, "Even though you have ten thousand guardians in Christ, you do not have many fathers, for in Christ Jesus I became your father through the gospel. Therefore, I urge you to imitate me" (1 Corinthians 4:15–16). On the basis of Paul's maturity and long-time relationship with the believers, he was able to urge them to imitate him.

The Apostle John addressed the older men in the church with these words: "I write to you, fathers, because you have known him who is from the beginning" (1 John 2:13–14). He recognized that they had known Jesus for a long time, and he instructed these older men, believers and followers of Jesus for many years, to recognize the rich gift of their experiences and wisdom. They were to draw on this wealth of wisdom and life experiences and use it to inspire and guide those who were younger in their life and in their faith journey.

When we consider Old Testament society, we recognize that God provided several groups to give leadership and direction. We normally think of the priests and the prophets, but there was another class of people who were an important part of Israelite society—the "wise men" or "sages." A reference to these three classes of people is given by those who opposed Jeremiah when they said, "Come, let's make plans against Jeremiah; for the teaching of the law by the priest will not be lost, nor will counsel from *the wise*, nor the word from the prophets" (Jeremiah 18:18, emphasis added).

In one of Ezekiel's words of prophecy, there is a sense of hopelessness and despair. The reason for the calamity is the people's conduct. As a consequence, there would be no guidance from God and no direction from the elders. Ezekiel prophesied, "Calamity upon calamity will come, and rumor upon rumor. They will try to get a vision from the prophet; the teaching of the law by the priest will be lost, as will the *counsel of the elders*" (Ezekiel 7:26, emphasis added).

The point is that God led his people through three groups—prophets, priests, and elders. The thrust of the Wisdom books of Proverbs and Ecclesiastes is words of wisdom from a father to his son. In Bible times, God provided "sages," "elders," and "wise men and women" as a critical class of leaders to guide his people. Similarly, in our modern world, God has given us elders, both women and men, to guide us as well. We need to affirm and hear the words of these elders because they have words of wisdom from God.

Today, we regrettably hear older people say that they have no value— or, at least, they feel that way. In Israelite society and in the early church, the assumption was that older people had value because they were older. It is no coincidence that an elderly couple, Zechariah and Elizabeth, were the first to hear about the conception of Jesus, the Messiah (Luke 1:35–56). It is also no coincidence that God so directed it that two elderly people, Simeon and Anna, were the first to see the baby Jesus in the temple and bless him and his parents (Luke 2:25–38).

The best hope for our country, our churches, and our families is to return to the biblical model and affirm the role and contributions of the elderly. "When one thinks of elders, one should not think of frail, dependent people. On the contrary, the hope of our nation and perhaps of the world rests on the shoulders of those who comprise the aging church. The most frail and physically dependent person may also be the most ardent prayer warrior or the most wise or courageous member of a congregation" (James M. Houston and Michael Parker, *A Vision for the Aging Church*, 124).

Reflections

Recognizing the wisdom seniors provide requires a response:
• As a senior: How do I show courage to accept my responsibility?

• As a non-senior: How do I humbly show that I receive the wisdom of seniors?

Prayer

Heavenly Father, as I come towards the end of my life, I look back with deep gratitude, remembering all the times you have carried me. You have been faithful, no matter what I was experiencing. Further, as I look back, I am also keenly aware that many people have walked with me. At times, I have felt alone, but in those times you provided family, friends, and the church, who lifted me and cared for me. And this is also the case now. I am not walking alone. At times, it feels that way. But you place caring people around me. I value them, and I want them to know how much they mean to me. Thank you for expressing your love through your people. This gives me hope. In Jesus' name, Amen.

Appendices

The central metaphor of this book is a marathon. The title, *Preparing to Cross the Finish Line*, emphasizes the importance of being ready for the moment we die. But, as has been emphasized throughout the book, there are specific things that can be done now to be better prepared for that time. In this appendix are various guidelines and forms that will help people in their preparation. Some of the forms will need to be adapted for the particular situation a person is at, as well as for where the person lives. Please take the time to review and, as you are able, fill in these forms or begin addressing the areas that apply to you.

Appendix A
Writing a Personal Life Story

1. Core Values in a Personal Life Story

Review the chapter on a life story (Chapter Ten: The Life Story: A Personal and Faith Legacy) and consider the following points.

• Our written life story can be perceived as our final life will. It includes the faith and the values we want to pass on to our children and the next generation.

• Our life story should begin with the basic facts of our lives but should also include times of God's miraculous intervention and restoration.

• The purpose of a life story is to bring glory and praise to God. A related purpose is that the people who read our story will receive hope and courage and encouragement for a renewed commitment to God.

• A core premise as we write our life story is that we have value. Our value is not based on what we have done, achieved, or accumulated, but on the fact that we are created in God's image.

2. Key Areas in a Personal Life Story

What are the areas you will want to include?

• *Family of Origin:* This might be perceived as establishing the roots that give us our identity. We want to note who our parents and earlier generations are. Our lives do not begin with us.

• *Childhood Events:* Here we mention special early events, both those pleasant and those painful. How were we nourished in our formative lives?

• *Milestones in Life:* Our lives are like journeys on which we encounter other people. We will begin by noting our relationships—our marriage, our children, other close family members. If we are not married or have no family, we will want to recognize other close relationships. We will also write about our education and the various areas of employment. If there has been a longer period in retirement, we will want to include special achievements or goals in our retirement.

• *Faith Encounters:* We recognize that the center of our lives is not ourselves but a caring and almighty God who has been present throughout all the phases of our lives. We have the opportunity to write our life story so that the focus is not on ourselves but on our God. Ultimately, our lives and therefore our life story must point to God. He gives courage for each day and hope for the future. May our life stories demonstrate how God is transforming us.

Appendix B
Forms Provided by a Church

This comment is regularly made when a family is in the midst of planning a funeral: "I had no idea how many things needed to be done. Planning a funeral is almost as complicated as planning a wedding, but a family has only a few days to get it all done." That is where a church and a pastor can be very helpful. I tell the grieving family that when they come into my office, it is a "one stop" arrangement. Then I, along with the office staff, will ensure that all the contacts will be made to individuals who are responsible for areas such as food, custodial, ushering, bulletins, music, and donations.

My church has developed four forms: a master planner containing all the details, a preliminary service order, a funeral catering menu, and a price list.

A few comments are in order as you study these forms. First, every church will have its own policies, traditions, and guidelines. The forms printed here are adapted from our church's forms, but much of the information will apply to other churches and even to a service in a funeral home. I encourage elderly people to meet with me to discuss their wishes, become familiar with the funeral service, and document their plans.

1. Master Funeral Planner
I begin by explaining the "Master Funeral Planner" with the family. This is a comprehensive form that contains all the necessary information and decisions a family will need to make as far as the church is concerned. The family will need to make other decisions with the funeral home. A family might not have answers for all of the various areas when they meet for the first time, but they will know what they need to work on as they plan the funeral.

FUNERAL PLANNER

Basic Information:
Name of Deceased: _____
Date of Birth: _____
Date of Death: _____
Place of Death: _____
Family Contact: _____
Phone: _____
Email: _____
Date of Death: _____
Place of Death: _____
Funeral Home: _____
Funeral Home Phone: _____
Funeral Home Contact: _____
Viewing Public/Private:
Date and Time: _____
___ Public ___ Private
Place of viewing: _____
Funeral/Memorial Service:
Date and Time: _____
Place: _____
Minister: _____
Church Involved: _____
Church Phone: _____
Service Broadcast: Yes _____ No _____
Via Livestream: _____
TV: _____
Other: _____
Burial: Yes ___ No ___ Cremation: Yes _____ No _____
Graveside Service:
Date and Time: _____
Cemetery: _____
Minister: _____
Parts of the Service:
Favorite Scriptures: _____
_____
_____
Music: Organ: _____ Piano: _____ Other: _____
Musician: _____ Phone: _____
Congregational Hymns: _____
_____

_____

_____

Special Music: _____

By: _____ Phone: _____

Pictorial Tribute:

By: _____ Phone: _____

Life Story/Obituary:

Prepared by: _____ Phone: _____

Read by: _____

Tributes:

1. By: _____ Phone: _____

2. By: _____ Phone: _____

3. By: _____ Phone: _____

Pallbearers:

1. _____ Phone: _____

2. _____ Phone: _____

3. _____ Phone: _____

4. _____ Phone: _____

5. _____ Phone: _____

6. _____ Phone: _____

Bulletin:

Prepared and Printed by:

Church _____ Funeral Home _____ Family _____

Picture(s): _____ Number: _____

Fellowship Reception:

Location: _____

Menu Selected: _____ Size of Family: _____

Total Number of People Expected: _____

Sharing Time after Meal: _____

Led by: _____

Display:

Location: _____

Obituary:

Printed in Denominational Periodical: _____

Printed in Local Newspaper :_____

Donations in Memory of/for: _____

Recordings of Service:

Includes Sharing Time: Yes _____ No _____

Number: DVD _____ USB _____

2. Preliminary Service Order

When I meet with the family, I will say, "I am here to help you plan a funeral service for your loved ones. My desire is that you will be involved in planning this service, and I will provide help wherever you might need and request it. I also recognize that you might never have planned a memorial service. This form provides a structure on how to plan a service." While I use a standard format, I also encourage the family to suggest changes, as long as they are appropriate and fitting.

However, I also realize that in many faith traditions the leader, be it a priest, a pastor, or some other member of the clergy, will have a clearly developed and accepted structure that is fairly standard and that there will be little input from the family.

A family will often ask how long a normal funeral service should be. My response is that the part of the service that will be shorter or longer is the family part. This includes the tributes by the children and the grandchildren, as well as the spoken and pictorial life story. When there are a larger number of grandchildren, I suggest that one or two speak on behalf of all the grandchildren, sharing stories and memories from those who will not speak in the service. I also state that the pictorial life story should not include all the events

Structure of the Central Funeral Rite
The Gathering
The Procession to the Front of the Church
Service of Prayer and Word
• Collect
• Prayer of Confession
• Scripture
• Sermon or Homily
• Naming and Witness
• Creed
• Prayers of Intercession
Holy Communion
Sending

from all the time periods in a long life. Having said this, I emphasize that the service will be the only one that the family will plan for their loved one. Therefore, I encourage the family to make it as special as they wish.

ORDER OF SERVICE
Organ/ Piano Prelude
Procession
Welcome and Prayer
Hymn
Special Music
Family Items
• Life Story
• Tributes:
    a. Children,
    b. Grandchildren

• Visual Life Story
• Other?
Message
Music
Hymn
Closing Remarks and Benediction
Recessional

3. Funeral Catering Menu

Each church will have its own practice regarding food services at a memorial service. The family for whom the service is planned might not be a part of the church where the funeral for their parents takes place. This means that they will not be aware of the practices of the church they are dealing with. We attempt to meet specific requests from the family, such as providing gluten-free baking or providing an item that was special to the family. Each church will have its own method of providing a luncheon or refreshments. A church form should include as many details as possible. The main concern is that we be clear and open regarding the food that will be provided and the cost.

4. Price List for Memorial Services

I believe it is important to be transparent and clearly explain the costs involved. The majority of families expect there will be expenses and will be satisfied with an explanation. Each church will have its own specific arrangements. It is crucial that these are understood. These are the items on our church's "Memorial Price List":
a. Bulletins
b. Catering
c. DVD recordings
d. Facilities—itemize the various areas if necessary
e. Custodial
f. Sound technician/PA

Appendix C
Legal and Financial Matters

The following comments will best be understood using the metaphor that this book is based on—our life is a marathon that we will finish as we cross the finish line. For some people, the marathon is brief, and for other people it is longer. However, at some point, each person will cross the finish line. Each of us

End-of-life decisions should not be made at the end of life.

has the choice—and I stress also the responsibility—to make decisions that apply both to the time before and the time after we die. Also, our choices deal with various matters. The book has dealt primarily with spiritual and relational matters. However, decisions will need to be made in other areas, including legal, financial, and medical matters. If you do not make these decisions, then other people will make them for you. Also, it is best that these decisions are made in consultation with your family members and/or close friends.

First, a word of caution: I am not a lawyer and cannot and do not provide legal advice. The contents of this section do not constitute legal advice, are not intended to be a substitute for legal advice, and should not be relied upon as such. The regulations in matters such as a power of attorney, a will, a representation agreement, and advance care planning will vary based on a person's province or state. Every effort has been made to ensure that the material is correct, but I cannot guarantee its accuracy or completeness.

Medical and health decisions will be dealt with in the next section. In this section, I will briefly discuss the legal and financial matters.

1. A Power of Attorney and a Will

A "power of attorney" is a legal document. It gives someone you trust the power to look after your property (your legal and financial affairs) if you are unable to do so. This might include paying bills, depositing or withdrawing money from your bank account, investing your money, or selling your home. There are distinctions between a "limited power of attorney" (restricting the appointed person's powers to a specific task or time period), an "enduring power of attorney" (giving the person authority which "endures" after you are mentally incapable, whether due to illness, an accident, or age-related decline), and a "springing power of attorney" (giving the person authority only after a "triggering event" such as two physicians declaring you to be mentally incapable).

The person you give this power to is called the "attorney." In this case, "attorney" does not mean "lawyer." It simply means the person you have chosen to be your decision-maker.

It is important to be aware of the differences between a power of attorney and a will. A "will" helps other people distribute your possessions after your death. A "power of attorney" helps you plan the management of your affairs during your lifetime. An "executor" is the person named in a will to carry out (execute) the instructions in the will after you have died. An "attorney" is the person responsible for your legal and financial matters during your life.

2. The Value of a Will

A will is a legal document that says what you want done with your property when you die. This property includes real estate, money, investments, and personal and household belongings. You can change your will at any time. A will has no legal effect until you die.

Every adult who owns assets or has a spouse or young children should have a will. If you don't have a will, you lose control over who gets your money and property, and when. You also give up the right to appoint a guardian for any young children you have. The costs to administer your estate will be much higher when you do not have a will.

A will doesn't deal with some types of property. A will generally doesn't cover property you don't own exclusively. For example, a joint bank account or a house owned in joint tenancy has a "right of survivorship." That means these automatically become the property of the joint survivor when you die. Also, a will does not apply to property such as life insurance, retirement savings plans and income funds, and tax-free savings accounts if you have already named a beneficiary for them.

If you pass away without having made a will, the law says how your property will get distributed and who has the right to administer your affairs.

3. Estate Planning

With estate planning, you might be able to reduce fees and taxes that your estate would otherwise pay. Consider, for example, the following strategies:

a. Joint Assets. These can include a joint bank account that two or more people own, or a home owned by two or more people as joint tenants. The owners of joint assets have a "right of survivorship." That is, the home is said to "pass outside your will" to the other joint owner.

b. Assets with a Designated Beneficiary. Registered retirement savings plans (RRSPs), registered retirement income funds (RRIFs), and tax-free savings accounts (TFSAs) all let you name a beneficiary who will get the proceeds when you die.

c. Life Insurance Policies. These let you name a beneficiary to receive money at your death. This money passes outside your will and does not go through the estate. This means the life insurance funds are not used to pay off the debts of the estate.

d. Trusts. Depending on the size of your estate, you might want to set up a trust (outside the will) to protect your estate against someone undertaking legal action to change some terms of your will (that is, making a wills variation claim).

e. Charitable Gifts. You can reduce the income tax owing from the sale of your assets on your death by making charitable gifts or bequests in your will. Here are several things to consider:
• You can reduce the income tax owing from the sale of your assets on your death by making charitable gifts in your will.
• The charitable gift might be a specific dollar amount or a percentage of the assets.
• A suggestion is to add another "child" in your will. By this I mean that if you have three children between which your estate is to be divided, then you can divide the estate into four units—each of the three children will receive one quarter, and the fourth child, your selected charities, will receive the other quarter.
• To leave a charitable bequest in your will, it is often best to use a public foundation such as Abundance Canada (www.abundance.ca).

4. The Importance of Getting It Right

There are good do-it-yourself materials available that can help you write a simple will. The will can take care of basic concerns, such as leaving a home, investments, and personal items to loved ones. However, you should be aware that there are rules and formalities that must be followed, no matter how simple the will. Otherwise, the will might not be valid.

A will is a legally binding document. Having your will prepared by an experienced estates lawyer or notary public is the safest way to avoid mistakes. Knowing your will is properly drafted can give you peace of mind. That way, you can be confident your affairs will be handled according to your wishes. To make an effective will requires a good understanding of property ownership rules and the laws about wills. The words used must be chosen carefully so that the will is clear. If the formalities are ignored or the terms of the will are unclear, there might be extra legal costs for your estate to get court orders to fix the problems—and in some cases, that might not even be possible.

Getting professional help is particularly important when there are features such as a blended family, a charitable gift, property outside the province or state in which you live, a family business, a desire to hold property in trust for someone (such as minor children), or a wish to leave certain people out of your will.

5. Choosing an Executor

When it comes to choosing an executor, you should choose someone you trust and who will likely be alive when you die. This person might be a trusted family member or friend. Often, people appoint their spouse, but if both of you are old, an adult child might be a better choice. It helps if your executor is well organized, good at keeping records, and a good communicator. Most importantly, the person must be willing to do the job as executor.

You can appoint more than one executor, and the executors can act together as co-executors. It's important to appoint an alternate executor, who can take over if the first executor can no longer act.

If you have a complex estate or investments or need someone to take over the operation of a company, you should consider naming a professional executor. This person might be a lawyer, an accountant, or another professional. Trust companies can also be the executor if the estate is big enough. Professionals and trust companies charge for their services.

6. Appointing a Guardian

If you are a parent or guardian of a minor child or children (under 19 years old), the law usually lets you appoint someone to be the child's guardian in your will. It is especially important to name a guardian if you are a single parent. For separated parents, it's best to agree on the choice of a guardian if one or both of the parents dies. If that's not possible, it's important to sort out the parenting responsibilities (through a court order or separation agreement) and ensure that the other parent is included as part of appointing a guardian in your will.

Although your choice of guardian is important, the court doesn't have to follow your wishes and might appoint a different guardian if it is determined that would be in the child's best interests. The court will consider the wishes of any child twelve or older, so you should check with older children about their wishes before deciding on whom to name as guardian in our will.

The guardian's job is to look after your minor children. The guardian might in turn appoint a replacement guardian. The guardian generally doesn't have any rights to look after a minor child's property. The guardian can only receive and hold a minor child's property or money if it's worth less than $10,000. If the child's property exceeds that amount, you should appoint a trustee to manage the minor child's inheritance. The executor can be the same person as the trustee.

It is helpful to create a trust to protect a minor child's interest in an estate. Make sure your will is written so that children under 19 won't have direct access to their share until they are 19 or older. If minors are entitled to a share in an estate and the will doesn't say that their share is going to be held in trust for them, the law usually says their share has to be paid to a Public Guardian and Trustee to be held in trust for the minor until the child is 19 years old. It is best to speak to a lawyer about drafting a trust.

7. The Importance of Preparation

You can minimize legal fees by preparing well.

You should have the following information ready before you meet with a lawyer or notary public about preparing your will:

• A list of everyone in your immediate family, with their full names and contact information, their relationship to you, and the ages of all your children, including stepchildren.

• The names and addresses of any other people or organizations you want to give gifts to.

• A list of all your assets and their values, including your home, your car, your investments, and any personal items of significant monetary value.

• A description of how you own these assets (for example, alone or with someone else).

• A document that shows whose name is on the title of any real estate you own.

• Details of any insurance policies your own and, specifically, the beneficiaries under the policies.

• Details of any pensions, retirement savings plans or income funds, and tax-free savings accounts, and who the beneficiaries are.

• Information on the structure of any business you operate (for example, a company or partnership).

• Any separation agreements or court orders requiring you to make support payments or dealing with guardianship of any minor children.

• The name, address, and occupation of your executor and guardian.

8. Filing a Wills Notice

A wills notice should be filed with the wills registry of your province or state. A wills notice says who made the will and where it is kept. This is a voluntary registration and has a small filing fee. The registry does not take a copy of your will. Instead, you or your lawyer or notary will fill out an information form listing where your will is kept. After you die, a search of the wills registry is required for the court probate process to ensure the court has the last will.

9. Review the Will

It's good to review your will every three to five years to ensure that it still reflects your current wishes. You should consider changing your will whenever your financial or personal circumstances change or if your beneficiaries die or reach the age of majority. For example, if you prepared a will when your children were young and named your parents as guardian and executor, you will no longer need the guardian clause when your children become adults. You might want your adult children or a sibling to be your executor instead. You should also review your will after any change in your marital status.

It is important to realize that your will can be changed after you die. If your will does not properly provide for your spouse or children (including illegitimate and adopted children), they can request to have your will changed by a court. This is called a wills variation claim. A "spouse" includes both a married spouse and a person you have lived with in a marriage-like relationship for at least two years before your death. The law is clear that you have both a legal and a moral obligation to provide for a spouse or child in a will. If you have a disabled adult child and do not leave enough for that child, the court might order that the child receive more from your estate. A lawyer can help draft an appropriately worded trust for a disabled adult child.

10. Keep the Will Safe

A common question is: "Where should I keep my will?" The answer is that you should keep the original will with your lawyer or notary or in a safety deposit box at your bank. That way, the will is in a permanent, safe, and fireproof location. Your executor will need your original will (not a copy) to give to the probate registry. You should let your executor know where you keep your will and other important documents, so the executor will know where to get it.

Appendix D
Health Matters

In the previous section, I noted that you are able to give directions regarding your financial assets through a power of attorney and a will. But these two documents do not pertain to medical matters. The following are several ways to safeguard your beliefs, values, and wishes regarding your health care treatments.

Advance Directive: This is a legal document setting out what actions should or should not be taken in regards to your health if you are no longer able to make or communicate decisions for yourself.

Representation Agreement: A representation agreement is a legal document to help you plan for your health and personal care. A representation agreement authorizes a person or persons to assist an adult with decision making (sometimes called supported decision making) or to make decisions on the adult's behalf (sometimes called substitute decision making).

Advance Care Plan: This is a verbal or written summary of a capable adult's wishes and instructions about the kind of care the person wants or does not want in the event that the person cannot speak for himself or herself. An advance care plan can be written down or simply told to someone who is authorized to speak for the patient, such as a substitute decision maker. It can guide a substitute decision maker if that person is asked by a health care provider to make treatment decisions on behalf of the adult.

Medical Order for Scope of Treatment (MOST): This is a doctor's order based on advance care planning conversations which explore your values and goals and the range of treatments available. This is a tool to communicate medical orders to health care providers and ambulance services.

Appendix E
Necessary Information

Throughout your life, you are making decisions, some minor and some major. It is necessary and helpful to have a process of storing and finding critical documents that is both straightforward and easy. This is important at all stages of your life but especially as you approach the end of your life.

There are decisions that pertain particularly to the last years of your life. Yet it is wise if these decisions are made earlier in life. These include decisions regarding your will, organ donation, a living will, a representation agreement, and funeral plans. The option is yours: you can choose to take care of these things when you can calmly make your decisions and then inform people what these decisions are, what the important information is, and where it can be found. If you don't take care of these items now, then these decisions will be made by your children or your spouse when they are in shock and grief. Also, if your will is not made, then the government will make decisions for you.

It is wise to have conversations with your children, or whomever you assign to be responsible for your life affairs such as your medical care, finances, and funeral plans.

Family members or whomever you assign as responsible for your funeral and your estate should be able to easily locate your important information. It is necessary to review your information on a regular basis.

It is also helpful to keep a copy of this information on a computer file where it can be easily updated. However, the most reliable and accessible form of information is paper—yes, paper—because when you have entered information using some software, it is not guaranteed that your children, or whoever wishes to access it, will have the necessary software.

Professional forms with these items are available from funeral homes, insurance companies, banks, lawyers, and financial advisors.

Also, some of this information will vary depending on the jurisdiction where you live. An example is that some provinces will have standard living will and representation agreements. Therefore, when a person moves, especially in the later years of life, this needs to be clearly understood. Also, the government policy that applies where the parents live might not be the same as the policy where the children live.

Important Documents and Decisions

❏ Vital Statistics

Name: _____

Address: _____

Phone: _____

Occupation, Title: _____

Birth Certificate: _____

Medical Care Card: _____

Social Insurance Number: _____

Veteran's Serial Number: _____

Date of Birth: _____

Place of Birth: _____

Canadian Citizenship Number: _____

Father's Name: _____

Father's Birthplace: _____

Mother's Maiden Name: _____

Mother's Birthplace: _____

Spouse: _____

❏ Will:

Lawyer: _____

Company: _____

Address: _____

Phone: _____

Email: _____

Person with Copy of Will: _____

Second Person with Copy: _____

❏ Power of Attorney:

Name: _____

Address: _____

Phone: _____

Email: _____

❏ Executor:

Name: _____

Address: _____

Phone: _____

Email: _____

☐ Living Will / Representation Agreement
Discuss with your family and doctor.

☐ Organ Donation
Individual decisions each of us must make.

☐ Life Insurance Policies
Insurance Co. #1: _____
Policy #: _____
Name of Agency: _____
Phone: _____
Name of Insured: _____
Beneficiary: _____

Insurance Co. #2: _____
Policy #: _____
Name of Agency: _____
Phone: _____
Name of Insured: _____
Beneficiary: _____

☐ Bank Accounts & Investments
Checking Account #1: _____
Institution: _____
Location: _____

Checking Account #2: _____
Institution: _____
Location: _____

Savings Account #1: _____
Institution: _____
Location: _____

Savings Account #2: _____
Institution: _____
Location: _____

☐ RRSPs, IRAs, 401(k)s
Account #1: _____
Institution: _____
Location: _____

Account #2: _____
Institution: _____
Location: _____

☐ RRIFs or LIFs
RRIF or LIF #1: _____
Institution: _____
Location: _____

RRIF or LIF #2: _____
Institution: _____
Location: _____

☐ TFSA
TFSA #1: _____
Institution: _____
Location: _____

☐ Other Investments:
Type of Account: _____
Account #: _____
Institution: _____
Location: _____

Type of Account: _____
Account #: _____
Institution: _____
Location: _____

☐ Deeds to Real Estate
If mortgage, #: _____
Mortgage Company: _____
Location: _____

Property Type: _____
Value: _____
Location: _____

☐ Credit Cards
Type of card: _____
Credit Card No: _____
PIN: _____

Type of card: _____
Credit Card No: _____
PIN: _____

Type of card: _____
Credit Card No: _____
PIN: _____

☐ Income Tax Returns
Account No.: _____
Location of papers: _____

☐ Marriage License
Spouse: _____
Where Married: _____
Date of Marriage: _____
Location of Certificate: _____

☐ Funeral - Preplanned
Funeral Home: _____
Location: _____
Funeral Director: _____
Choice: Embalming: Yes___   No___
               Cremation: Yes___   No___
Cemetery: _____
Location: _____
Contact Phone: _____

☐ Funeral Service - Preplanned
Church: _____
Location: _____
Telephone: _____
Email: _____
Pastor: _____
Phone: _____

☐ Family - Names & Addresses
☐ Children
Contact #1: Son: _____ Daughter: _____
Name: _____
Address: _____

Phone: _____

Email: _____

Contact #2: Son: _____ Daughter: _____

Name: _____

Address: _____

Phone: _____

Email: _____

Contact #3: Son: _____ Daughter: _____

Name: _____

Address: _____

Phone: _____

Email: _____

Contact #4: Son: _____ Daughter: _____

Name: _____

Address: _____

Phone: _____

Email: _____

❏ **Grandchildren**

    Contact #1: Male: _____ Female: _____

    Name: _____

    Address: _____

    Phone: _____

    Email: _____

❏ **Sisters and Brothers**

❏ **Cousins**

❏ **Nieces and Nephews**

❏ **Friends - names & addresses**

Appendix F
Definitions

Burial Service: also known as a "committal service," where the body or cremains (ashes of a loved one) are committed to the ground or final resting place.

Casket: a chest or container intended for treasured items. When this word is used in the funeral context, it certainly implies that the body is treasured.

Catafalque: a wooden stand or metal support on which a coffin or casket is placed.

Coffin: comes from the Greek word "*koffinos,*" meaning a "basket." This is a long, narrow box, often tapered at both ends, in which the body of the deceased is placed.

Columbarium: an above ground structure in a cemetery where urns containing cremated remains can be placed in small compartments or "niches."

Committal service: This service has two meanings: a service in which we commit the body or the ashes to the ground as well as a service in which we commit or entrust our loved one to God.

Cortege: a solemn procession, traditionally the procession of mourners traveling on foot behind a vehicle conveying a body in a casket or coffin. The cortege will proceed from the place where the funeral ceremony was held to the place of burial.

Crematorium or Crematory: a venue for the cremation of the dead. In many countries, crematoria contain facilities for funeral ceremonies, such as a chapel.

Eulogy or Life story: The word *"eulogy"* is a compound word consisting of *"eu"* (meaning "well, good") and *"logos"* (meaning "word"). "Eulogy" and "life story" can be used interchangeably. A life story begins with the basic facts that comprise an obituary. Then, various elements are expanded upon, and personal reflections or memories are added.

Funeral Service: the traditional and accepted name for the gathering to remember a departed person.

• **Memorial Service:** a service in which we thank God for the memories of a loved one. This service will normally be without the body of the deceased.

• **Celebration of Life Service:** a service to celebrate the life of a person. When this is a Christian service, the purpose will be to celebrate God's faithfulness in the life of a loved one.

Funeral Celebrant: a person trained and certified to provide a funeral, memorial, or celebration of life service that is highly personalized to reflect the personality, lifestyle, and beliefs of the person who died.

Interment: the act of interring or burying. The English word "inter" comes from the Latin *"in"* (meaning "in") and *"terra"* (meaning "earth"). Therefore, "interment" refers to placing a body "in the earth."

Mausoleum: an above ground structure in a cemetery where caskets are placed in specially constructed compartments called "crypts."

Obituary: a short account of a person's life that includes key events. This is the brief write-up that will be used for a local newspaper or other media.

Tribute: A tribute consists of words of appreciation for the life and the achievements of a loved one. The purpose of a tribute is to share specific memories and express how the loved one left a positive impact on the life of the person giving the tribute.

Appendix G
Selected Books on Aging and the End of Life

Aging/Funerals/Dying

Billings, J. Todd. *The End of the Christian Life: How Embracing Our Mortality Frees Us to Truly Live.* Grand Rapids, Michigan: Brazos Press, 2020.

Breuhaus, Betty. *When the Sun Goes Down: A Serendipitous Guide to Planning Your Own Funeral.* New York, Lincoln, Shanghai: iUniverse Inc., 2007.

Callanan, Maggie, and Patricia Kelley. *Final Gifts: Understanding the Special Awareness, Needs, and Communications of the Dying.* New York: Simon and Schuster, 2012.

Cullen, Lisa Takeuchi. *Remember Me: A Lively Tour of the New American Way of Death.* New York: Harper Collins, 2006.

Craddock, Fred, Dale Goldsmith, and Joy V. Goldsmith. *Speaking of Dying: Recovering the Church's Voice in the Face of Death.* Grand Rapids, Michigan: Brazos Press, 2012.

Dugdale, L. S. *The Lost Art of Dying: Reviving Forgotten Wisdom.* New York: Harper One, An Imprint of HarperCollins Publishers, 2020.

Fournier, Elizabeth. *The Green Burial Guidebook: Everything You Need to Plan an Affordable, Environmentally Friendly Burial.* Novato, California: New World Library, 2018.

Gordon-Lennox, Jeltje. *Crafting Meaningful Funeral Rituals: A Practical Guide.* London and Philadelphia: Jessica Kingsley Publishers, 2020.

Habenstein, Robert W., and William M. Lamers. *Funeral Customs the World Over.* Milwaukee: Bulfin Printers, 1963.

Hauerwas, Stanley, Carole Bailey Stoneking, Keith G. Meador, and David Cloutier, eds. *Growing Old in Christ.* Grand Rapids, Michigan: William B. Eerdmans Publishing Company, 2003.

Herring, Lucinda. *Reimagining Death: Stories and Practical Wisdom for Home Funerals and Green Burials.* Berkeley, California: North Atlantic Books, 2019.

Houston, James M. *Joyful Exiles: Life in Christ on the Dangerous Edge of Things.* Downers Grove, Illinois: IVP Books, 2006.

Houston, James M., and Michael Parker. *A Vision for the Aging Church: Renewing Ministry for and by Seniors.* Downers Grove, Illinois: IVP Academic, 2011.

Lane, Annette M., and Marlette B. Reed. *Making Meaning in Older Age: Bringing Together the Pieces of Your Life.* Winnipeg, Manitoba: Word Alive Press, 2017.

Long, Thomas G. *Accompany Them with Singing: The Christian Funeral.* Louisville, Kentucky: Westminster John Knox Press, 2013.

Long, Thomas G., and Thomas Lynch. *The Good Funeral: Death, Grief, and the Community of Care.* Louisville, Kentucky: Westminster John Knox Press, 2013.

Moll, Rob. *The Art of Dying: Living Fully into the Life to Come.* Downers Grove, Illinois: InterVarsity Press, 2010.

Mitford, Jessica. *The American Way of Death.* New York: Simon and Schuster, 1978.

Nouwen, Henri J. M. *Our Greatest Gift*: *A Meditation on Dying and Caring.* New York: HarperCollins Publishers, 1994.

Packer, J. I. *Finishing Our Course with Joy: Guidance from God for Engaging with Our Aging.* Wheaton, Illinois: Crossway, 2014.

Perry, Tim. *Funerals: For the Care of Souls.* Bellingham, Washington: Lexham Press, 2021.

Schmidt, Alvin J. *Cremation, Embalmment, or Neither?: A Biblical/Christian Evaluation.* Bloomington, Indiana: WestBow Press, 2015.

Schmidt, Alvin J. *Dust to Dust or Ashes to Ashes? A Biblical and Christian Examination of Cremation.* Salisbury, MA: Regina Orthodox Press Inc. 2005.

Stevens, R. Paul. *Aging Matters: Finding your calling for the rest of your life.* Grand Rapids, Michigan, Cambridge, U.K.: William B. Eerdmans Publishing Company, 2016.

Swinton, John, and Richard Payne, eds. *Living Well and Dying Faithfully: Christian Practices for End-of-Life Care.* Grand Rapids, Michigan: William B. Eerdmans Publishing Company, 2009.

Verhey, Allen. *The Christian Art of Dying: Learning from Jesus.* Grand Rapids, Michigan: William B. Eerdmans Publishing Company, 2011.

Grief and Sorrow
Billings, J. Todd. *Rejoicing in Lament: Wrestling with Incurable Cancer and Life in Christ.* Grand Rapids, Michigan: Brazos Press, 2015.

Hastings, W. Ross. *Where Do Broken Hearts Go? An Integrative, Participational Theology of Grief.* Eugene, Oregon: Cascade Books, 2016.

Manning, Doug. *Don't Take My Grief Away from Me: How to Walk Through Grief and Learn to Live Again.* Oklahoma City, Oklahoma: In-Sight Books, 2005.

Sleeth, Matthew. *Hope Always: How to be a force for life in a culture of suicide.* Carol Stream, Illinois: Tyndale Momentum, 2021.

Zylla, Phil C. *The Roots of Sorrow: A Pastoral Theology of Suffering.* Waco, Texas: Baylor University Press, 2012.

Financial and Medical Decisions
Abundance Canada (www.abundance.ca).

Foster, Sandra E. *You Can't Take It with You: Common-Sense Estate Planning for Canadians.* Mississauga, Ontario: John Wiley and Sons, 2007.

My Voice: Expressing My Wishes for Future Health Care Treatment. British Columbia Ministry of Health (healthlink.bc.ca), 2020.

Wark, Kevin. *The Essential Canadian Guide to Estate Planning: A Journey towards Peace of Mind,* 2017.

Restoring Relationships

Bevere, John. *The Bait of Satan: Living Free from the Deadly Trap of Offense.* Lake Mary, Florida: Charisma House, 2011.

Carlson, Dwight L. *Overcoming Hurt and Anger: Finding Freedom from Negative Emotions.* Eugene, Oregon: Harvest House Publishers, 2000.

Johnson, Richard P. *How to Honor Your Aging Parents: Principles of Caregiving.* Ligouri, Missouri: Ligouri Publications, 1999.

Kendall, R. T. *Total Forgiveness: When Everything in You Wants to Hold a Grudge, Point a Finger and Remember the Pain—God Wants You to Lay It All Aside.* Lake Mary, Florida: Charisma House, 2002.

Lederach, John Paul. *The Journey Toward Reconciliation.* Scottsdale, Pennsylvania; Waterloo, Ontario: Herald Press, 1999.

Nori, Don. *Breaking Generational Curses: Releasing God's Power in Us, Our Children, and Our Destiny.* Shippensburg, Pennsylvania: Destiny Image Publishers, 2005.

Palmer, Parker J. *A. Hidden Wholeness: The Journey Toward an Undivided Life; Welcoming the Soul and Weaving Community in a Wounded World.* San Francisco: Jossey-Bass, 2004.

Pritchard, Ray. *The Healing Power of Forgiveness.* Eugene, Oregon: Harvest House Publishers, 2005.

Seamands, David. *Healing of Damaged Emotions.* Wheaton, Illinois: Scripture Press, 1981.

Walters, Trevor. *EAS Syndrome: Healing Burnout in Adults Lacking Parental Affirmation.* Newport Beach, California: Anglican House, 2016.

Wilson, Rod J. K. *Counseling and Community: Using Church Relationships to Reinforce Counseling.* Thomas Nelson, 1995; Vancouver, British Columbia: Regent College Publishing, 2003.

Endorsements

"Some 500 years before Christ, Heraclitus wrote, 'No man ever steps into the same river twice, for it is not the same river and he is not the same man.' In *Preparing to Cross the Finish Line*, Pastor Walter Wiens is acutely aware how very fast-moving societal shifts in our time impact all of life, including the planning of memorial services. Evident is the author's long experience in walking with families in their grieving while sensitively dealing with complex issues. In addition to reflecting a rich pastoral experience, *Preparing to Cross the Finish Line* embodies wide consultation and extensive reading. Entrenched in this book is a comforting spirituality variously expressed, including a prayer at the conclusion of each chapter. Readability is enhanced by numerous insets with thought-summaries or theme-related citations. Perhaps the greatest strength of this publication is the author's continuous use of Scripture as central to planning memorials in ways that encourage both worship and healing."

– David Giesbrecht
Abbotsford, B.C.

"In a society that seems to reflect less on the aging process and the inevitability of each of us dying, *Preparing to Cross the Finish Line* reminds us of the reality of death and the importance of preparing for it and helping our families and others around us do the same. It does so in an engaging way as each chapter ends with thought-provoking questions and helpful next steps. The writer's lengthy experience and passion for end-of-life issues makes it a must read."

– Dwayne Barkman, retired pastor,
Warman, Saskatchewan

"I have had the privilege of working with Pastor Walter Wiens as a funeral director in the Abbotsford community for many years. He and I have served together helping hundreds of families, and I have always appreciated his passion for this particular part of pastoral ministry. It is appointed unto man once to die, yet our society behaves as though we will not. Pastor Walter brings his experience to bear as he discusses the details that should be considered by families as they prepare to honor their loved one. He has done an excellent job of covering all of the thorny issues that can come up at the time of death, including family dysfunction."

– Jonathan Chapman, funeral director
Abbotsford, B.C.

"A few years ago, I lost my father and father-in-law in the space of six weeks. One funeral to plan and execute, a brief reprieve, and then another one. I think we did okay, but I can see now how beneficial it would have been to have had this wisdom-packed book for guidance. Walter Wiens shows us the importance of funerals and memorial services, uncovers how funeral planning can be tricky with remaining family members, and gives us many practical checklists that will make planning more simple and meaningful. His compassionate pastor's heart shines through as he shares many stories of families who faced difficulties in the process. His chapters on recognizing family brokenness and restoring peace in relationships are very beneficial. I highly recommend this book."

– Lando Klassen, founder of House of James bookstore
Abbotsford, B.C.

"*Preparing to Cross the Finish Line* takes us on a comprehensive journey through the 'end of life' concerns here on earth. This is a sensitive and thought provoking read."

–Lorraine Dick, Care Ministry Assistant,
Clearbrook Mennonite Brethren Church, Abbotsford, B.C.

"Pastor Walter Wiens has spent a lifetime in compassionate caring ministries. In *Preparing to Cross the Finish Line*, he has given those facing death and their families relevant, essential, clear guidance on death and dying. I know Walter as a friend and fellow pastor and am thankful for the helpful wisdom he so willingly shares. Since death is an everyday reality for all of us, I see this as a book every family will want to possess to guide them through those times.

– Norm Miller,
retired pastor, college president, professor, chaplain, and engineer

"As a health care worker in a care home during the COVID-19 pandemic, I spent much time with the residents, caring for them, liaising with their families, and being present at their bedsides as they passed away. In this book, the inner brokenness and unresolved issues that many of us privately carry are openly validated, affirmed, and given a voice; there is a courageous and refreshing removing of the religious veil covering up our damaged, vulnerable, grieving selves; and there is a compassionate acknowledgement of personal wounding, often resulting in deeply seated, distorted concepts of God. Yet, with humble sensitivity, an open door of hope is offered, allowing a freedom to openly express real, honest emotions and dialogue in a safe, secure environment. Ever so gently, one is drawn to a place where almost even "angels fear to tread, a place of personal encounter with a deeply compassionate, loving, caring God, a God, who knows, sees, and understands it all, a God who wants to comfort and heal our broken hearts. With much sensitivity, the urgent issue of broken relationships is clearly addressed, calling for courage to leave a legacy of reconciliation and restored peace. From the most dedicated church leader to the 'ordinary Joe,' from the completely unchurched to the aging senior, this book graciously offers a place of acceptance, recognition, and help in our common humanness and frailties. It provides a welcome rest for one's soul as we, together, 'Prepare to Cross the Finished Line.'"

– Vi Wiens
Health care worker in care homes

"The decisions and demands presented at the death of a loved one are myriad. These come when we are least able to face them. It is better to be prepared with forethought and intentional values. Pastor Walter Wiens offers us a guide which enables us to do now what we will have to do later. I encourage all readers to not only read these pages, but to also accept the wisdom and support they contain. I know Pastor Wiens to be a caring, thoughtful voice for end-of-life matters. He is effective in writing of things we tend to ignore. You will find his work to be detailed, pragmatic, and effective for the family walking through loss."

– Scott Tolhurst, former Pastor of Clearbrook Mennonite Brethren Church,
Abbotsford B.C.

www.ingramcontent.com/pod-product-compliance
Lightning Source LLC
Chambersburg PA
CBHW080957120626
46546CB00010B/2940

* 9 7 8 1 9 9 8 7 8 7 0 1 2 *